A House Restored

A House Restored

THE TRAGEDIES *and* TRIUMPHS *of* SAVING *a* NEW ENGLAND COLONIAL

Lee McColgan

Foreword by Roy Underhill

Countryman Press

An Imprint of W. W. Norton & Company
Independent Publishers Since 1923

To Liz,
the one I write for

Contents

Foreword

Architecture is frozen music.

—*Johann von Goethe*

ACCORDING TO LEE McCOLGAN, "IN A NEW England winter, Colonial architecture is frozen pipes" and, may I add, all the joy that goes with that! Who wouldn't prefer snaking through an icy crawlspace under an ancient kitchen floor, towing ribbons of heating tape to defrost the pipes, rather than sitting in yet another meeting? I've been in that spidery crawlspace many times—because they're universal—delighted not to be sitting in an office, while still wondering how long it would take before they found my body. But that doesn't matter. It's our house now, with all its drafts, rattles, creaks, and bug-eaten timbers, and the work ahead will make it our home.

An ensemble of workers wielding trowels, axes, planes, and hammers first played the frozen music of the Colonial-era Loring House, the subject of this adventure. Lee McColgan, new owner of this old, old house, faces a choice as he tackles the restoration: Should he take the easy path and inject modern methods and materials into the piece, striking the inevitable false notes, or was it possible in these times to "get the band back together" and play the old music on the original instruments? Fortunately for us, McColgan chose to honor the old-hand ways and sought guidance from the living masters of these timeless trades of the building arts. It's the hero's journey played out in fieldstone and oak.

McColgan's teachers are legends, aristocrats with calloused hands. Top timber-framer Michael Burrey shows the ways of the mortise and tenon. Olivia Morland of the Worshipful Company of Plaisterers places a trowel in Lee's hands and sends him in search of the elusive Fabio, keeper of lime and goat hair. Through the squint of blacksmiths, McColgan learns to read the glow of wrought iron in the eye of the fire. He tames the mighty drystone and learns to knife window putty to weatherproof perfection. Each master imparts a gift to aid our hero in his quest.

Even with all this help, McColgan's preparation for the challenge began long before confronting the Jabberwock of the Loring House. At every turn, we see the power of an adventurous childhood, a confident self-reliance imbued from a time when no one said, "You can't do that." *Can I build that tree house? Can I make this powder explode? Can I make this light come on? Yes, yes, yes, I can.* The adventurous spirit starts young and lasts a lifetime.

Broadaxe, limestone, all of it seems very old, but it will carry on well after our passage of petroleum and plastic has ended. McColgan's materials are organic. His wooden windows, so excellently glazed—what a proper word for puttying glass into place—will never choke a sea turtle with broken-down vinyl bits. His hewn oak beams will sequester carbon for centuries. He himself has grown stronger and his world saner. Even if all this axe-wielding and stone rolling represent just spiritual redemption by ancestral tokens—folks, it's just what we need!

As master housewright at Colonial Williamsburg, I studied the surviving evidence (documents, buildings, tools) and worked to replicate historical building techniques as well as the missing buildings in town. Because so many of the old buildings had been restored fully, the old work covered over long before I arrived, our studies of the untouched, original carpentry often took us into steamy attics and creepy crawlspaces. But the clues were there, grace notes in the old beams and bricks, places where a diamond-shaped depression made by four chisel cuts preceded old auger bits because they had no lead screws at that time. Mysterious cross-hatchings atop a timber finally revealed themselves as the places where the long-ago carpenter sat and pointed his pegs to lock the joints into place. Slowly the truth of the system, the harmonious whole, resonated as we brought each note from the past into the present, sounding it on the broadaxe, the tucking trowel, the putty knife, and the final grind of a settling fieldstone.

We can learn to play the old music, but sometimes we shouldn't. In Williamsburg, we seldom participated in restoring the old buildings. Just as when conserving a valuable painting, the ethic is *not* to use old materials to make undetectable repairs because future investigators might mistake your replacement work for the original. (A bit of vanity assumes that your work is that good.) But worse than confusing the evidence is destroying it. Repointing a weathered brick wall must be undertaken with the old, soft lime mortar because modern, hard cement will cause the old bricks' faces to spall away quickly.

So what to do? Like restoring that valuable painting, you make sure that your work on the old house is reversible, that you use compatible materials, that you preserve as much of the original as possible, and that you leave good indications of your contributions. You place a coin from the year of your work down in a mortise. You scratch a date in a corner of the plaster. Better yet, you write a book about it! Thank you, Lee, for letting us take part in your adventure. You gave us a vision for the grand journey and the courage to undertake it.

—*Roy Underhill*

Introduction

We can make our lives sublime,
And, departing, leave behind us
Footprints on the sands of time.

—Henry Longfellow

I N THE SUMMER OF 2015, WHILE I WAS ON THE road in Lincoln, Nebraska, a phone call informed me that my morning meeting had been cancelled. For several years, a large investment firm employed me as a representative assigned to their Midwestern territory, meeting with financial advisers in the region to sell more of the company's products. With time to kill before my next meeting, I bought a coffee at a local bakery and sat in the car, sipping it, watching as other customers came and went. Looking aimlessly out the window, my eyes wandered to a sign planted in the front yard of a plain, brick building across the street.

OPEN HOUSE
Sand mandala viewing
All are welcome.

Inside, the sweet smell of lavender hung in the air. A man wearing a button-down shirt tucked into a pair of khakis greeted me. "Come on in," he whispered, handing me a pamphlet. "Sit anywhere you like."

Perched on wooden benches lining the walls, small clusters of people gazed at the scene in the center of the room. Monks crouched on the floor, huddled around a large blue board inscribed with an intricate geometric pattern. The men wore long robes the color of cranberries from bogs dotting the landscape of Massachusetts, where I had lived before moving to the Cornhusker State. The freely flowing fabric contrasted starkly with the sharp lines of my white collar, the perfectly centered dimple in my necktie, and the crisp crease of my suit pants. The occasional cough or low murmur punctuated the quiet.

Each monk carefully held a chak-pur, a copper funnel filled with colored sand ground down from precious gems and stones. The men tapped the funnels gently, distributing the grains in delicate lines, like pâtissiers piping icing onto a sheet cake. Their hands moved with smooth deliberation and incredible control.

Reading the pamphlet, which my own hands had been gripping tightly, the paper now creased, revealed that these Buddhist monks had traveled from Tibet to demonstrate the ancient art of mandalas, spreading their philosophy across the globe. For a week, they spent untold hours painstakingly creating the design and forming the pattern with just a few grains of sand at a time. When they finished, they swept up the sand and poured it into a river, an Etch A Sketch from the ancient world. The mandala represents the universe and the cycles of creation and destruction within it. The artwork and its fate remind us that nothing in life is permanent. The practice of sand painting trains the monks to release their attachments to earthly objects—to art, beauty, even the results of their labor—and to accept that everything exists in a constant state of change. In theory, accepting this impermanence makes it easier to endure loss.

The outline on the board slowly disappeared under little piles of vibrant sand that brought the geometric pattern to life. The granulated material gave texture to the design, like the wool pile of a patterned rug. The slow, deliberate movements transfixed me. But a nagging sense of time passing pulled me from the trance into which the demonstration had drawn me. Wanting to be on time for my next meeting, I slipped out the door, quickly forgetting the experience and returning to my routine, those few contemplative moments sinking deep into the recesses of my mind.

BY 2020, my career in finance had yielded to a life dedicated to preserving historic buildings, one of which I had had the good fortune to buy. A contractor hired me to help restore windows, and working for his clients filled my days, while working on my own house filled my nights. That blazing summer, Boston's Old North Church—where lanterns famously signaled whether British forces were coming by land or sea—hired us to restore some of their windows. We removed them in stages, transporting them for repair in a small shop in Halifax, near Plymouth, then drove them back to the North End for reinstallation.

On a blistering August Monday, I pulled onto a street so narrow that I had to collapse the delivery van's side-view mirror to keep it from scraping a narrow gauntlet of cars and buildings. Once a home for Italian immigrants, the North End has become an affluent destination renowned for its restaurants and bakeries. In the air, the savory smells of pork roasting with a licorice hint of fennel mingled with the rich, sugary scents of chocolate and vanilla. From the age of industrialization, scarlet brick buildings stood watch over the street, their copper gutters and flashing oxidized to the same blue-green as the Statue of Liberty.

The church's windows—stacked precariously behind me, at the hurried request of my employer, but separated with insulation foam—rattled as the van navigated bumps and potholes. A deep rut in the pavement suddenly appeared, causing me to stomp the brake pedal and spin the steering wheel hard to the left to avoid it, but it was too late. The front of the van dropped with a *thump*. It was a relief to see, over my shoulder, that none of the glass had broken.

With the hazards flashing and the van wedged in a parking spot reserved for emergency responders and garbage trucks, I delicately unloaded each window in a perilous race to get them safely back into the church before a parking ticket spoiled the run. In the grueling dog-day heat, a steep flight of stairs brought me and the windows up to the second story. It was going take several days to reinstall them all.

That night, at home, there was no time for rest. Fatigue had soaked into my bones, but my own old house, built twenty years before the Old North Church, needed work, too. In the kitchen, workers long ago had removed a section of wide pine floorboards when installing an HVAC vent. They replaced the original hand-planed pine with narrow boards of factory-cut wood, the grooves running perpendicular to the rest of the floor, the lines completely askew. Then they covered the entire floor with linoleum.

An old nail puller with a slide hammer and small jaws pried the nails from the patch where the vent lay. The little metal spikes screeched as they emerged, their shafts bending from the pressure. A pile of mangled fasteners grew around me as I worked. It was a simple task, but control of the tool demanded complete focus. With repetition, the motions became automatic. The smaller boards came up, and new planks—wide pine cut at a local sawmill—gently replaced them, each piece fitting perfectly as it had in the beginning. The careful work engrossed me until the sun was sliding into the horizon. By 9 p.m., the lack of natural light made it difficult to see, and exhaustion made it hard to continue. Drained, I sat on the stairs leading to the second story.

For months, living and breathing preservation had consumed me. My hands had grown calloused, hard like the chew toys that Bryson, my black Labrador retriever, liked to gnaw. Constellations of cuts and knicks appeared in assorted stages of healing, scar tissue building where various knuckles had lost layers of skin. The constant movement of my hands split new layers faster than my body could repair itself. Under the surface of my left thumbnail, a bruise had bloomed, orchid purple, where a hammer had careened onto it a few days earlier. As I bent forward to collect a scrap of wood from the floor, pain shot through my right knee. The tendons and ligaments felt as if they were shredding like paper. I crumpled back down on the stairs, the room dark and silent. Then the Buddhist monks emerged from the depths of my memory.

In the years that had passed, an idea had swept me up, a belief in the righteousness of preservation. Saving historic buildings was *good*. In my view, their lifespans should measure in centuries, defying the impermanence of the universe, which I didn't want to accept for them or for myself.

A strange thought occurred to me. Alone in my kitchen, I realized that everything I had been doing, the purpose to which I had dedicated my life, was running perpendicular to the philosophy of those holy men who created beautiful works of art only to destroy them. I wanted what I built to *last*. But no one can escape fate. On a long enough timeline, my house and I will disappear, eroded into infinity, washed away like sand into the river of time. Following this thought came a nagging question. Why did saving this old building, *any* old building, matter?

The answer revealed itself slowly in the history of the

house and the work that went into making it last. The original craftsmen and even their names had disappeared, as would my own contributions, but the work endured for a time. Preserving the beauty and utility of the structure connected me to the past. Mixing plaster became a meditation, as did honing wood and carefully setting stones like lines of sand. The contentment of working with my hands and the peace of a job well done—saving a dwelling that sheltered the body, pleased the eye, and fed the soul, though all transient—provided a path from the past through the present into the future.

The house helped me find meaningful purpose. The work taught me about construction techniques and building materials and how both have evolved, changing the nature of the places we inhabit. These subtle details affect how we feel when driving down a street, pulling into a driveway, or walking through a door, no small matter. After all, we spend most of our lives at home. Most profound, though, was the realization that through architecture we can project ourselves into what we build, which is why our homes tell us something about who we are. In understanding my house, I came to understand a little more about the world and myself.

A House Restored

I.

A Place to Call Home

The house is not merely a possession or a
structure of unfeeling walls. It is an extension
of my physical body and my sense of self that
reflects who I was, am, and want to be.

—*Karen Lollar*

ALL MORNING, THE SWELTERING SUN HAD
been beating onto the roof. The steel of the crowbar already felt warm. My arm strained, wedging
the feathered end of the tool between the seam of two veneer
panels nailed to a kitchen wall. With more pressure, the nails
loosened, one panel lifting. Cracking, its edge popped open.
Particles of dust floated in the air, dancing in the sunlight,
tingling my nose, and making me want to sneeze. The smell
of aged wood, the yeasty aroma of freshly baked bread, filled
the room. In just twenty-four hours, guests were arriving.

Almost immediately the house had made life difficult.
Inadequate light from small windows made it hard to see.
The ceilings hung so low that, when standing, the top of
my head almost touched the plaster. Door frames hung low

too, more problematic because their position caused frequent collisions when rushing through the house. If I didn't duck fast enough or had a ball cap on, the brim obstructing my view, my forehead cracked into the wood, which left a throbbing purple welt above my eyes. The door frame at the bottom of the main staircase proved worst, gravity causing me to build speed while descending so the impact came at maximum velocity.

From centuries of settling, most of the door frames had subsided out of square, and many of the doors no longer closed properly. Around exterior doors, light shone through tiny gaps during the day, and cold drafts infiltrated at night. When the wind blew, the windows rattled. The floorboards pitched and rolled, tossing me around as though on a ship in rough seas.

Whenever it rained, the house soaked up water. The whole building felt sticky inside. Humidity warped the books in the study, and mildew grew on the walls. At one point, the atmosphere inside the house grew so damp that a stack of envelopes glued itself shut. Absorbing the moisture, the floorboards swelled. When they dried, they shrank back down, squeezing the nails holding them in place, dislodging the nail heads and lifting them out like pulling a splinter. My socks snagged on them, tearing holes that damaged them beyond saving. Periodically, I grabbed a hammer and played whack-a-mole, hunting down as many as I could find. Stubbing a toe or stepping on one had more severe consequences. I kept my tetanus booster up to date.

The house itself faced constant attack, too. Carpenter ants infiltrated a bathroom. A swarm of termites appeared at the back door. Wasps descended from the attic, disrupting meals. Rodents clawed their way inside. No matter how many holes I plugged, rodents kept coming, their transportation network rivalling that of the Roman Empire. When one perished under the floorboards, the house filled with the sickening, musty smell of rot. Snakes slithered into the basement to find a dry and warm home in the openings between the stones in the foundation. At all hours of the night, mysterious scratching emanated from the walls. A family of opossums moved in, which we discovered when, for several days, our cat pawed at the corner of the room above the cellar.

Those plagues of creatures and other inconveniences to daily living formed only part of the problem. The number of repairs seemed endless. When I fixed one thing, something else went wrong. Every day became a fight to stave off deterioration, the house crumbling faster than I could work. It felt like patching leaks in a dam during a thunderstorm with a constant feeling of dread that, at any moment, the whole thing would give way, swallowed whole by the maelstrom. The repairs were consuming all my time and money, the latter always near the root of any argument with my wife, Liz. I loved the house, but it was ruining my life.

Standing in the kitchen, holding the crowbar, I paused. All around, construction debris lay strewn in piles on the floor. The idea of tearing out the 1970s veneer panels and

restoring the original 1700s woodwork once seemed gratifying, thrilling even. But after more than a year of work—in
which every small project somehow became a big one—
what lurked behind the veneer worried me. So much still
needed doing, and I was running out of time. I wiped my
brow with my free hand, centuries-old dust mixing with
sweat and leaving a black smudge on my face. Sitting down
on the stairs, I thought, *Why did I ever buy an old house?*

A COUPLE of years earlier, on a clear spring morning, we
turned down Old Bay Path, a quiet country road running
through the South Shore of Massachusetts. The trees had
started budding, heralding a new season. Liz stared out the
passenger window, scanning the numbers on each mailbox
we passed.

"Up here, take a left!" she shouted.

Past a circular driveway, a wall of shrubs and crooked juni-
pers hid the house, like a lost city waiting to be discovered.

"This is it," she said.

We sat for a moment, taking in a vast expanse of horse
pasture that extended to a dense forest. A solitary pony
grazed picturesquely in the distance. In a nearby patch of
wetland, frogs croaked their chorus. A modern suburb
had sprung up around the property, but it still felt isolated,
peaceful except for the sound of the occasional passing car.

The large house had two stories and simple, rectangular
geometry. The pitched roof made the building look like an

oversized version of a hotel from *Monopoly* but with two chimneys, one at each end. Like locks of hair, the weathered shingles had faded from the blond of freshly cut cedar to silvery gray. On the gable end of the house, the panes in the two windows reflected the sky like twinkling blue eyes. They shot me a glance from across the yard.

Over the centuries, the house had declined. The roofline sagged where no underlying rafters supported it, and elsewhere the exterior showed evidence of botched work. But it still drew me in. The proportions of the windows and doors gave it a pleasing, unique style. Visions of how it might have looked when new drifted through my head. It had an adorned simplicity, plain S-curve moldings constituting most of the trim, except for the woodwork surrounding the main door, which demonstrated the meticulous craftsmanship of the period. Flanking that door stood two large, fluted pilasters topped with an intricate, molded pediment, all inspired by Roman architecture, a miniature wooden Pantheon in relief. The façade faced south, into the direct path of the sun's warmth. Even then, builders knew the importance of energy efficiency.

Despite the charm of the original entryway, the side door's proximity to the driveway made that entrance more convenient. The approach led down a long, handlaid brick walkway. We followed it, brushing away thick patches of vegetation growing over the path. Liz dashed past me with the key, fiddled with the deadbolt, and pushed the door open. The view from the threshold revealed that most of

The front door of the Loring House.

PHOTO BY ARI KELLERMAN.

the architectural updates had ceased in the mid-1800s. It felt less like entering an old house and more like entering another time.

An aged, woody fragrance washed over us, a hint of smokiness from centuries of logs burning in the fireplace, like the rich aroma of a peaty Scotch. The low ceilings made me feel like a giant: Gulliver entering a strange new land.

"What do you think?" Liz asked.

A smile crept onto my face. It was exactly what I'd been seeking.

At the dawn of the 1700s, builders had erected the house for Thomas Loring III. Originally a single-story home—two main rooms, hall, parlor, and fireplace—it had grown as successive generations of the Loring family acquired wealth and expanded the structure's footprint. One story rose to two. An addition on the east elevation doubled its size and added another chimney. Off the back, a later addition created an L, against which a shed now huddled. Stitched together like a patchwork quilt, various pieces merged and combined, creating a labyrinth through time that added an air of mystery to the place. The rooms represented different moments in the evolution of the house, each an escape from the ordinary. The doorways between most of the small rooms aligned, so standing at one end of the house gave a clear sight line to the other, creating a clever illusion of more space. Each rectangular opening resembled a painting on the wall. It felt like you were stepping into the canvas of a masterpiece hanging in a museum.

With childlike wonder, we strolled through the house, marveling at what appeared around each corner. In addition to hidden closets and secret doors, a small compartment in an upstairs bedroom lay concealed under floorboards painted to hide it. The thick beams of the house's frame protruded from the finished surfaces, as if seeking attention. Pine boards encased parts of the beams, while others stood exposed, festooned with scalloped indentations where a carpenter's axe had cut them square. Workers had planed the wood by hand, producing slightly concave tracks where the plane's iron had passed. The secret tracks revealed themselves only when the sun shone on them at just the right angle. Countless layers of paint had split and cracked in places, weathered like an old face.

Unlike new residential construction—all clean edges, everything plumb—nothing in the Loring House sat true to square. The pine floorboards, some three feet wide, led us through each space like a designated pathway. In the dining room, one of them felt springy and let out a feeble groan. The nails had released their grip, the board no longer fixed to the underlying joist. The long plank flexed under my weight like a diving board.

Over every finished wall and ceiling lay a thick coat of creamy plaster. Its surface had tiny pits and hollows, but from across the room the swathe of white concealed their presence. Instead of knobs, the doors featured wrought-iron latches covered in tiny dents that recorded the blows of a blacksmith's hammer. Pressing the thumb lever of a closed latch revealed a staircase to the attic, an unfinished space divulging the bones of the building. Across the room stretched rows of rafters, the house's giant ribcage. Between them stood the two brick chimney stacks, which rose from the rooms below, continued through the roof, and opened into the sky. Looming like ancient sentinels, the stacks towered above the house to carry their dangerous cargo of smoke and embers far away from the inhabitants' lungs and dried wood inside the building.

After a few minutes, I made my way back to the lower level, stopping to observe, through one of the old sash windows, the pasture behind the house. Tiny furrows and bubbles in each pane of glass, the result of hand-blowing, obscured the scene. Through blurred panes, the world looked different. The view reminded me of the duality in which we see buildings as part of our setting, but they also offer vantages from which to behold other settings. A bird arced across the sky, and the landscape contorted through the imperfections, melting together like wax.

In the living room, the bricks of the great fireplace, still charred with ash, had slight irregularities in shape and size. The brickmakers had molded them by hand and fired them in a wood-burning kiln. The flue's wide opening shrank as each layer of corbeled bricks gradually narrowed, constricting the air flowing into the atmosphere, creating a draft, and preserving the heat in the room. Looking up into the darkness, the abyss gazed back down at me, a black hole that might suck me in. From under the opening, I stood up, dusting soot from my hands, and continued wandering. Nearby stood a small door. A blast of cool, musty air rose from below as its hinges creaked open, revealing another ancient wooden staircase, this one leading to the cellar.

Flicking on a light switch, I descended, ducking my head and clearing cobwebs as I made my way underground. The house sat on a foundation of individual fieldstones, a rough assortment of shapes and shades of gray, each placed methodically. The entire structure consisted of porous, permeable materials that strategically allowed it to breathe. Every space had recesses, pockets, nooks, crannies. Nothing about it had the flat sterility of new construction. Texture rioted everywhere.

Before the dawn of the Industrial Age, laborers had constructed the house with basic tools and materials created with minimal processing. Primitive, the building offered refuge from the whipping winds of winter, shelter from the searing summer sun, and defense from the drenching of heavy downpours. But it did so at a cost to itself, enduring relentless exposure to the same elements against which it protected its inhabitants. Made to outlast its builders, it still had its own lifecycle. The indifferent natural world that had produced the resources for its construction fought constantly to reclaim it. A clear compromise accompanied the prospect of owning it: This place to call home came with the ongoing responsibility of maintaining it. Delaying its deterioration soon became my goal. By signing the contract to purchase the house, I had no idea that I'd just made a deal with the devil.

WHEN I was ten years old, my family moved from a Boston suburb to Rutland, Vermont, a small city surrounded by mountains rolling in all directions. Bobby Newbury, one of my childhood friends, lived on a farm abutting undeveloped land on the edge of town. One Saturday morning, he and I hiked past a gravel pit, its crushing machines connected by the long tongues of conveyer belts, the landscape punctuated with water holes filled with cattails, marsh grass, and peeping frogs. We climbed a hill, debris tumbling down the embankment with each step, to a path through thorny brush and wildflowers. Just beyond rose a row of spruce, maple, and hemlock, all standing guard. Beneath their canopy, we left behind open, dry land and entered the woods. In the cool, damp air, mosquitoes and gnats hovered in clusters around us. Dense layers of moss and fallen leaves carpeted the forest floor, making the ground feel spongy. Large ferns surrounded us. It felt as though we had crossed into another dimension.

Several miles into the forest, a large boulder stood in a clearing where old trees had fallen. Round except for one side sheered flat, the standing stone looked like it didn't belong, as if it had landed there from outer space.

"Let's make a lean-to against that rock," I said to Bobby.

We gathered fallen branches, assembling them against the flat side of the stone in a neat row. We stripped hemlock saplings of their boughs and piled them atop the frame, weaving them together to keep them in place. With smaller stones, we constructed a fire pit inside, sealing the rocks into place with riverbank clay as mortar. The structure blended seamlessly with the environment. You could have walked past without noticing it at all. Far from adult supervision, free from the restrictions of school and our parents, we were creating our own roof, under which *we* made the rules.

At school the following Monday, class felt confining, and doodling endlessly on a piece of paper offered me an escape. By the time the bell rang, the entire palm of my right hand had smudged gray, the graphite from the pencil rubbed to a low luster. In art class, sitting high on stools, we worked with clay. Shaping figures on the table made me feel like some great god from Greek mythology. The joy of working with these simple materials felt primal, satisfying.

But college led me away from creative endeavors. A degree in business management helped me land a job selling investments. It paid well, which, for a young man with no money, provided its own satisfaction. A desire for advancement compelled me to create a new identity. A sales coach advised me to analyze my language and fight the tendency to say "um" and "like" when speaking. Recordings of my sales presentations allowed me to study my movements and gestures, like a coach reviewing practice footage before a game, which taught me how to use nonverbal signals to influence an audience. My wardrobe gained expensive charcoal-colored suits, pressed white-collared shirts, and conservative ties mostly in red or blue. A clean-shaven face eyed me in the mirror, hair combed to one side, each strand held firmly in place with an assortment of pastes and pomades.

The business world reshaped and remolded me. New mannerisms spilled into all areas of my life, affecting how I answered the phone and talked to friends and even family. All actions became calculated, robotic. Occasionally, my old clothes emerged from the depths of my dresser to help me tackle some weekend project, but my creative self largely went dormant.

Over time, though, a void formed inside me and grew, one that no amount of money could fill. "Pursue your passion, and the money will come," leaders in the business world had intoned, but the grapevine shared stories of people making big life changes that didn't go so well. One colleague left the industry to write a children's book, sinking money into graphic design work and self-publishing, but the story never took off. Another left the business to launch a restaurant but had to shut it down less than a year after opening. In the back of my mind lurked a concern that a quarter-life crisis was manifesting, something that would pass, and that waiting it out made for the best course of action. Still, something felt broken.

Then a friend gave me *The Framed Houses of Massachusetts Bay, 1625–1725*, a gift found at a flea market. A clear plastic jacket over the large, cherry red cover sounded like leaves rustling when it opened. Harvard University Press had published it in 1979, and in it architectural historian Abbott Lowell Cummings catalogued the earliest surviving English houses in Massachusetts, invigorating the preservation movement in America. The book contained detailed illustrations and photographs of many surviving first-period houses—floorplans, framing, chimneys, interiors, exteriors—with an entire chapter dedicated to the builders and their resources. Cummings paid special attention to the Fairbanks House, the oldest surviving house in the country, which today sits nestled among new construction in Dedham, a middle-class Boston suburb. The house's floor plan consists of simple squares and rectangles, which nonetheless required master craftsmen to build. Plain but possessing a crude refinement, it looks not unlike a barn. But the images captivated me, spurring me to Dedham—recruiting my father-in-law, Mark, to tag along—to tour the house museum and learn more about its construction.

We arrived early and waited outside with a few other visitors, the air already thick with humidity. A man emerged from an outbuilding and lumbered slowly down a short walkway across the yard.

"Welcome everyone," he said, breathing heavily, when he reached us. Sweat dripped from his face and blotted the fabric under his armpits. "Please follow me." Pulling a small key from his pocket, he jiggled it in the lock, opening the door, then squeezed through the narrow frame, the darkness of the interior swallowing him whole. The group trailed him, single file, encircling him in the entryway.

"Right now, you're standing in the oldest surviving house in the United States," he said, his voice shaking, eyes cast to the floor. "It was built by Jonathan Fairbanks in 1637."

As he told the story of the first owners, reciting a well-rehearsed script, my attention turned to the house itself, my eyes inspecting every room from floor to ceiling, trying to figure out how each part had been made. The large hewn beams looked like trees that had fallen in the Vermont forest, the bark dried and sloughed off. Workmen had caked plaster to the walls like mud. The foundation consisted of common stones that could've been gathered nearby. In many ways, it reminded me of the crude lean-to Bobby Newbury and I had built as kids.

A dawning sense of inspiration urged me to visit other historic houses: the Winslow House in Marshfield, built by the grandson of Edward Winslow, an elder passenger on the *Mayflower*; the House of the Seven Gables in Salem, made famous by Nathaniel Hawthorne's novel; Arrowhead, where Herman Melville wrote *Moby-Dick*. Apathetic tour guides kindly allowed me to poke around exposed framing in attics and foundations in basements, which showed me what made each house unique. Returning to these houses multiple times gave me a familiarity with them, making them old friends. A few years of crawling around museum houses brought me to a single-minded conclusion: I had to have one of my own.

Daydreams of buying an old house and fixing it up waltzed through my mind. Working with my hands—hammering nails, plastering holes, painting walls—would offer a welcome change from staring at screens or making more sales calls. The time had come to roll up my sleeves and get dirty. A sense of meaningful purpose had eluded me, but this idea felt right. All I needed to do now was find the right house.

Many early colonial houses stand scattered across New England. But most people balk at the inconveniences of living in period houses, modifying them to suit modern tolerances and tastes. Low ceilings come out to create more head space and wall storage. Plaster walls yield to drywall that can conceal electrical wires and modern insulation. Energy-efficient windows and doors replace their drafty predecessors. Often, after decades of remodeling and renovating, nothing original of a house remains but the frame.

Liz began following the real-estate market, sending listings whenever suitable prospects might have the early, unaltered craftsmanship that called to me. When something looked promising, she barraged the real estate agent with emails and calls, often racing out to see the properties as soon as they hit the market—but nothing felt like a good fit.

The wilderness still called to me. "Go out upon that, build yourself a hut, & there begin the process of devouring yourself alive," transcendentalist poet William Ellery Channing had told Henry Thoreau before the naturalist set out for Walden Pond. But moving too far from civilization would isolate us. Passing moods of introversion papered over the social creature that lay at my core. We needed a house where we could bring people together, celebrating with friends and family. The home had to have its own meaningful purpose beyond just fulfilling my desire to be a maker, and preserving it needed to achieve more than just curating an antique. We had to enjoy the lives we lived under its roof.

"I think I found it," Liz said one day. The Loring House gave her a warm feeling as soon as she walked into it. "It was as if we'd lived there our entire lives," she later said. Still, purchasing a 300-year-old house terrified us. We feared expenses from unexpected repairs and problems no doubt hiding behind every finished surface. But astonishingly it came with thirteen acres of land. That detail also appealed to local developers, who could demolish the old house, replace it with row after row of new construction, and make a considerable profit.

Concerned that someone else would snatch it up, we submitted an offer.

PRESERVING THE house mattered to us, but we also needed a change. Corporate life had made me sedentary. Whole days passed sitting in cars and office chairs. The muscles in my neck had knotted into a lump, and each morning, as I went to work, my stomach sank. The stress was making me irritable, and Liz was feeling it, too. She had grown up in a small town, riding horses as a child, and she also craved a simpler life. We daydreamed together about life on the Loring property, imagining growing vegetables, raising chickens, maybe even stabling and riding a couple of horses. We had an idyllic, admittedly naïve idea of the whole thing, but the final decision wasn't ours to make.

The outcome depended on Lydia Hale, who was selling the house. A small woman in her nineties, she had short, curly, gray hair. Her back had hunched with age, and she needed help walking. Her wrinkled face and hands looked like the weathered grain of the house's old wood, and they, too, contained a storied past. A Boston debutant, she reportedly danced with John F. Kennedy at a ball once, but she never saw herself as belonging to high society. She loathed formal schooling and grudgingly graduated from Concord Academy, a private school in the town where the American War of Independence began. When she married her second husband, her parents recoiled because he had no ties to the upper-class circles in which they moved.

More than anything, Lydia liked working with her hands. She built fires in the home's open hearth, spun wool, knitted sweaters, tended her gardens, split and stacked wood, cut the lawn on a John Deere riding mower, and even hand-laid the brick walkway from the driveway to the side door. Above all, she loved her animals—goats, sheep, horses—and had served as president of the National Pygmy Goat Association, publishing the group's newsletter from her dining room table.

But repairs to the house often took a back seat. "There was a funky swimming pool," her son David said. "She had it filled in. It was the only major change she made to the property in thirty years."

Nonetheless, Lydia cared deeply about the house and remained unwavering about its preservation. She had worried that vibrations from large trucks would rattle the foundation stones loose and lobbied the select board until they prohibited trucks above a certain weight from using the road. She made repairs only when necessary, trying desperately to avoid making unwarranted changes. She also didn't want developers to demolish the house.

Our real estate agent suggested that, with our offer, we include a personal note to her. The note mentioned Liz's love for horses and my passion for old houses. It promised we never would develop the property, divulging that we were as adamant about preserving the house as she was. The letter made it OK for Lydia Hale to let go.

We met for the closing in a modern office building in an industrial park not far from the house. Clinging to her daughter's arm, Lydia refused to use a wheelchair. She walked into the room, frail but defiant. She'd lived in the house for so long because it anchored her life. Recalling that life made her happy. But she was growing more forgetful, a risk for living alone, and the upkeep had become too much of a burden. So she moved in with her daughter and put the house on the market.

"I was so afraid to sell it," she said, "but then I read your letter."

Joined by her four children, we sat around a conference table as lawyers summarized stacks of papers teeming with legal jargon and minutiae. For Liz and me, the occasion crackled with the excitement of new beginnings. But Lydia and her family of course had mixed emotions. Her children smiled somberly as they recounted stories of their mother's life on the farm. They would miss the house, yes, but they were happily surrendering maintenance of it, which they'd taken over from their mother.

Lydia expressed a kind of joyful melancholy. She had found someone to continue her legacy of preserving the house, but she still didn't want to give it up. Sitting up straight, she took three items from a canvas bag and placed them on the table: a photo album of all the farm's animals from over the years, a bird's nest containing several tiny blue eggs, and a faded manila folder thick with papers and wrapped tightly with string. She gave me the album and nest, then pressed her hand on the folder, her arm shaking, and slid it across the laminated tabletop.

"Open this when you get back to the house," she instructed.

Then she put her name to the final page of the contract, signing with a grace that masked a deeper sadness. In that moment, her home became our home.

I walked from the conference room, my arms overflowing with stacks of legal paperwork topped by her gifts. The bird's nest, perched on top, began to slide. Before I could stop it, it slipped from the pile. In a second that felt like hours, it hit the ground, and the eggs tumbled out, every one cracking into little pieces. The gift, a symbol of a new beginning, now felt foreboding. In time, this misfortune would prove fitting.

Luring me with its beauty, the house had bewitched me. As soon as we moved in, problems emerged. Builders had constructed the house from the six main materials of the pre-industrial age: wood, plaster, iron, stone, glass, and brick. All of them had deteriorated, worn down for three centuries. Within every enchanting space lurked elements that needed repair. Everywhere, chipped paint was flaking, some of it in large patches that were peeling off like sunburned skin. Bricks had disintegrated into little piles of crimson dust. An overhead beam in the kitchen contained hundreds of tiny holes from a burrowing insect, giving it the appearance of Fontina cheese. Most of the glazing that held the glass panes in the window sashes had crumbled and vanished. Many of the panes themselves had cracked. Most of the iron hardware on the doors had rusted. Much of the plasterwork had hairline fractures from end to end. In some places, it had fallen off in chunks, exposing the wall's interior. A large brown stain had leeched into the ceiling near one of the chimney stacks. Even the modern utilities looked problematic. The walls between rooms consisted of nothing more than planks covered in lath and plaster, with nowhere to hide the twentieth century additions. Electrical wires crept down the walls from the attic like tendrils of some terrible vine. Exposed water lines ran overhead.

All these necessary repairs broke the spell that the Loring House had cast. A not-so-fine line runs between aging with grace and structural condemnation. The restoration had an urgency to it, but I didn't want to rush. I couldn't. The goal was to make repairs to preserve the house's character, but at this point I didn't know how.

There also were subtle differences among restoration, conservation, and preservation to consider. Restoration entails bringing a house back to how it looked when first built, with everything new, but different parts of the Loring House had gone up at different times, so every addition needed a different approach, which would complicate the work. Conservation calls for retaining the maximum amount possible of a house's original, unaltered material, prolonging the structure's life through carefully planned interventions that later hands can reverse without affecting the condition of that material. Conservators who handle priceless paintings, dissolving years of accumulated grime or patching tears in canvas, make those kinds of minimal changes. Preservation involves keeping a house as is, making no changes at all. The directors of the Aiken-Rhett House Museum in Charleston, South Carolina, for example, had left the interior of that structure completely untouched. Its paint and plaster flake, strips of peeled wallpaper hang loosely, and every surface shows the stains of history. Walking through it feels like floating through the rooms of the *Titanic* at the bottom of the Atlantic. In the Aiken-Rhett House, everything has stopped in time.

The Loring House needed a little of all three approaches: restoration, conservation, and preservation. If the roof was leaking, for example, leaving it untouched would constitute an act of gross negligence. Even if I did subscribe exclusively to the purist form of preservation, it made no sense to do nothing at all. A leaking roof would jeopardize the rest of the house. If the roof were to spring a leak, I'd have to restore the shingles to save the whole house.

Soon after builders finished work on the structure, it began to change, which holds true for all buildings. Architecture roots itself in permanence, so architects design buildings *not* to adapt, according to Stuart Brand in *How Buildings Learn: What Happens after They're Built*. As a result, most don't adapt. In constant flux, their environments and uses become a thorny challenge for restorers, who wrestle with decisions made long ago for remote reasons. "You can't fix or remodel an old place in the old way," Brand writes. "Techniques and materials keep changing. Factory-hung windows and doors are better than the old site-built ones, but they have different shapes. Sheetrock replaces plaster; steel studs replace wood. You have vapor barriers, plastic plumbing, plastic electrical fixtures, a dozen new forms of insulation, track lighting, task lighting, up-lighting, and carpet by the acre." This paradox was becoming my own challenge, and any decision affected the building's future and mine in it.

First order of business: figure out what techniques and materials to use. In the 1700s, building techniques looked fairly straightforward. Without electricity, builders used simple hand tools. Remnants of these techniques remain today, but the twentieth century brought dramatic change. In 1921, President Warren Harding appointed Herbert Hoover his secretary of Commerce. Hoover thrust housing into the national spotlight because he viewed homebuilding as a driving force for the economy. America couldn't boost the number of homeowners, he believed, unless the nation produced houses more efficiently by enabling builders to operate on larger scales. He followed in the successful track of Henry Ford, embracing the efficiencies of factory-line production.

By July 1950, Hoover's grand idea reached a new zenith. That month, *Time* magazine ran a cover story about a modern housing development named Levittown, near Hicksville, Long Island, New York, that employed a new method of building residential structures. "The most conspicuous Levitt innovation involved the division of the construction process into twenty-six tasks, each performed by a different crew of workers. Since each crew did the same job over and over again, the work went amazingly fast. In many cases, the crews simply installed fixtures or pieces prefabricated in a central shop, so only a few of the crews required highly skilled laborers," writes environmental historian Adam Rome in *The Bulldozer in the Countryside*.

Today, complex machinery makes and assembles components for most houses. In mills and factories around the world, deafening machines churn out a soulless parade of identical parts and pieces, belching the smell of petroleum-based lubricants. Tethered to assembly lines, factory workers keep dangerous equipment at a distance for fear of losing limbs or life amid mind-numbing repetition. Sometimes robots do the work, and technicians merely monitor the machinery.

On building sites, mixing trucks tumble concrete like dirty clothes in a washing machine and contractors pour the gray slurry to form foundations. Shipped on flatbeds like patients transported on gurneys, preassembled components arrive at the jobsites. Workers fasten them into place with pneumatic tools that sound like assault rifles, the *pop-pop-pop-pop-pop* echoing like suburban guerilla warfare. Conventional construction today rarely involves even simple tasks such as hammering nails or cutting wood. Entire houses rise at breakneck pace. These kinds of modern tools and techniques could have made restoring the Loring House a breeze, but they would have detracted from the house's character. The beautiful imperfections of skilled craftsmanship by hand made the house unique.

The minimally processed resources of the 1700s also looked fairly straightforward. The most advanced supplies then came from kilning or furnacing raw materials, which turned shells to plaster, clay to brick, sand to glass, and ore to iron. Processing, done by hand, made use of local resources. After refinement, the materials still somewhat resembled their natural forms.

But plastics changed everything. The word "plastic" conjures the Great Pacific Garbage Patch, a terrible gyre of ocean debris wreaking havoc on marine life. Here, dead fish, when cut open, spill horrifying plastic waste from their guts. So there's a particularly distasteful irony in plastics stemming from a desire to preserve the natural world. In the mid-1800s, all materials with the commercial properties of today's plastics came from animals. Finding alternatives meant ending a massive scale of slaughter. In the 1860s, amateur chemist John Wesley Hyatt created a natural polymer from the cellulose in cotton—a whitish material with the consistency of shoe leather—and called it celluloid. Unlike wood, which rotted when wet; metal, which corroded; rubber, which grew brittle; and ivory, which discolored, celluloid remained relatively unchanged when used.

"As petroleum came to the relief of the whale, so has celluloid given the elephant, the tortoise, and the coral insect a respite in their native haunts, and it will no longer be necessary to ransack the earth in pursuit of substances which are constantly growing scarcer," Hyatt hastily proclaimed.

Celluloid paved the way for a new breed of building materials. The first synthetic plastic made entirely in a laboratory, Bakelite soon followed. Scientists and engineers considered the patented, name-brand plastic a huge improvement on polymers found in nature. From that point, they stopped looking for materials to emulate nature and sought to rearrange nature itself in new and imaginative ways.

In the early 1900s, the rise of the petrochemical giants brought more innovation to the field of polymers. Oil refineries generate unwanted byproducts, but many of those byproducts contain the raw ingredients for polymers.

Ethylene gas can become polyethylene, the main ingredient in home water-shield products, such as Tyvek or ProArmor. Polyvinyl chloride (vinyl for short) helps create siding, windows, and flooring. Polyurethane goes into adhesives, paints, and finishes. The modern building-supply store contains endless iterations and permutations of plastic.

For the Loring House, two questions faced me: First, are modern materials *better* than traditional ones? Second, was it possible to fix the house the old-fashioned way? Modernization certainly has its benefits. Plumbing, electricity, heating, and air conditioning all made living in the house tolerable. But over time, many materials in remodeled areas of the home had revealed their flimsiness. The kitchen cabinets consisted of pressboard, or sheets of wood chips glued together. Installers then glued the countertops on the lower cabinets, but that adhesive was failing. It looked like stale chewing gum stuck to the underside of a high school desk.

Drywall, a lightweight plaster sandwiched between pieces of cardboard or paper and sold in four-by-eight-foot sheets, covered the new walls. Tapping on one of them produced a faint reverberation, a hollowness. *Easy enough to push my entire arm through it*, I thought. By contrast, the plaster-and-lath walls in the older, untouched parts of the house felt dense and hard, like brick. Even the traditional materials used in the newer parts of the house exhibited subtle differences. The house's original wooden boards ran more than one inch thick. At the lumber yard today, boards listed as "one-inch thick" run only three-quarters of an inch, patently false advertising that everyone knows and blithely accepts.

Modern materials also produce a different aesthetic. "You can't fix or remodel an old place in the old way," Stuart Brand had written—but why not?

The manila folder that Lydia Hale had given me contained various documents about the house: hand-written notes, photocopies, newspaper clippings, magazine articles, and photos that spanned a century or more. I assumed that Thomas Loring III had built the original structure himself, but no evidence indicated that he had any experience as a builder. The local historical society—a sleepy organization run by a handful of volunteers from a nineteenth century schoolhouse in the center of town—confirmed when Loring purchased the land, but they had no information about who built the core house. They directed me to a database filled with images of original documents pertaining to eighteenth-century carpenters working in the area. Most of the information had come from court proceedings, relating to debts owed on various construction projects, written in period English that was difficult to decipher.

A belief still persists that early Massachusetts colonists built their own houses, every farmer his own carpenter, but that belief is false. Records show that towns across the English colonies employed all manner of professional artisans. As today, those professionals often divided duties among themselves—carpenters, joiners, blacksmiths, masons—but many individual craftsmen could build a house from start to finish: Yanks of all trades, if you will. They did most of the work with a few simple tools. "The very simplest houses at Massachusetts Bay were carpenter-built, and carpenters loomed from the start as one of the largest groups of building artisans," writes Abbott Lowell Cummings. Yet little has survived about those individual builders or their stories. Like so many in America, their history has fallen into the margins. Whenever they appear in records, they go unnamed, denoted only by their trades. Some were skilled and some unskilled; some free, some indentured; some worked full-time, and some part-time. They toiled hard, raised families, and died in comparative obscurity. Time has forgotten most of them.

One of the few surviving personal accounts of a tradesman from the 1700s concerns master builder Richard Macy, parts of which appear in *Away Off Shore* by historian Nathaniel Philbrick. In that book about Nantucket Island and its people, Philbrick devotes a chapter to Macy, who at an early age apprenticed to become a house carpenter. Philbrick quotes Macy's grandson, who wrote:

> His practice was to bargain, to build a house, and finish it in every part, and find the materials. The boards and bricks he bought. The stones he collected on the common land; if they were rocks, he would split them. The lime he made by burning shells. The timber he cut here on island. The latter part of his building, when timber was not so easily procured of the right

dimensions, he went off island and felled the trees and hewed the timber to the proper dimensions. The principal part of the frames were of large oak timbers, some of which may be seen at present day. The iron-work, the nails excepted, he generally wrought with his own hands. Thus being prepared, he built the house mostly himself.

Reading that passage gave me an idea. I could do the restoration work at the Loring House myself, performing the repairs as a craftsman from the first period would have done. Self-reliant like Richard Macy, I would become a maker again, preserving the house's character that had becharmed me. From the long-ago words of a man remembering his grandfather, my plan took shape. To succeed, I needed to learn how to work with the house's basic materials: wood, lime, iron, stone, glass, and brick.

Eager to start, I laid out each step and talked through it with Liz. We set the dining table with our wedding china, ate dinner, and pored over the details, our nightly meals transforming into planning sessions. Books about building soon crowded my shelves, holding me rapt late into the night along with online research. The project was coming together.

Then one night—

"There's something else I want to talk about," Liz said, a serious tone in her voice.

"Sure, what is it?"

"I floated the idea of hosting next year's Thanksgiving,"

she revealed. "Our house would be perfect for it, and everyone is really excited. What do you think? Can you get the house ready?"

I pondered the question for a few seconds. "Of course, I can, no problem!"

Surely, I'd be able to figure it out, and eighteen months gave me plenty of time.

What could go wrong?

II

A Reverence for Wood

These woods are lovely dark and deep,
But I have promises to keep
And miles to go before I sleep.

—*Robert Frost*

ORK BEGAN IN THE KITCHEN. OVER THE years, the room had undergone remodeling many times, each alteration adding layers of new material, but the updates halted in the 1970s, as confirmed by then-popular dark brown veneer panels covering every conceivable surface. Like a fossil, the original structure lay buried somewhere beneath. Nailed in sheets to the walls, the veneer mimicked individual boards. Only the large timbers, left exposed, escaped this treatment, with the exception of one dubious corner entirely covered in veneer. A few basic tools—crowbar, hammer, utility knife—would help me to restore it.

Light cosmetic work, nothing more, I told myself. The house had different plans.

Wedging the crowbar under the seam of two panels,

steady pressure pried one of the sections off. The intersection of large, hefty beams, all coming together to form a neat corner, should have appeared; instead: nothing, an ominous void. The timbers had rotted away completely. Mere nubs of beams protruded from the walls, chewed like stumps near a beaver dam. Bugs had devoured the corner, turning it to dust and riddling the remaining wood with bore holes. Those remains felt spongy, like foam, some parts disintegrating before my eyes.

My mind raced, a dizzy feeling of panic overtaking me. The frame supported the massive weight of the house, but a corner of it was floating in thin air, a ghost. What was keeping gravity from crushing us?

Dropping the crowbar, which clanged on the floor, I dashed to the barn loft for scrap wood to use as supports. Rummaging through the pile, I threw pieces aside. Two sturdy-looking four-by-four fence posts appeared under some old planks. With one under each arm, I ran back into the house and propped them under what remained of the frame, still worried that the whole house might come crashing down at any moment.

First project: repair the timber frame.

"TIMBER FRAMING" describes the skeleton of a building made of large wooden beams, their ends cut to form interlocking joints. Today, most carpenters build house frames with pine two-by-fours or two-by-sixes bought from a local lumberyard, nails joining the soft boards together. Derisively called "balloon framing"—the joke being that a stiff breeze might blow the entire frame away—this faster, cheaper method first appeared in the 1830s. Because it required less skilled labor and supplied a burgeoning population more efficiently, it quickly became the industry standard.

The carpenters who erected the Loring House preferred dense, rot-resistant white oak. They would have felled trees on site, the chopping sounds of their axes echoing through the countryside, followed by the whoosh of leaves, snapping branches, and a reverberating *thud*. On the ground, their broad axes hewed the logs, squaring them into beams measuring eight-by-eight or more.

To form the interlocking joints, the workmen used saws, chisels, and auger bits to cut mortise-and-tenon joints, which connect in the same way that a plug fits into an electrical outlet. The workers hollowed a recess, the mortise, in one beam, then cut the end of a second beam into a tenon, the corresponding prong. They test-fitted each joint to ensure a smooth, secure fit. Then they drilled a hole through the joint and drove a wooden peg into it to hold everything in place. This method uses no nails but takes more time than the balloon framing of modern construction. That increased effort pays off in the long run because timber framing results in more durable structures. The Jokhang Monastery in Lhasa, Tibet, the world's oldest surviving timber-frame structure, has stood since the 600s CE.

From soup to nuts, building the frame of the Loring

House would have taken a year or more. A handful of carpenters could have fashioned the individual pieces, but raising the whole heavy frame required the entire community. In rural Pembroke, at the turn of the eighteenth century—long before phones, television, computers—raising served as an occasion for entertainment, bringing often isolated households together. Dressed formally, townsfolk and farmers made their way on foot or by horse and carriage to the site. With refreshments laid on linen-covered tables, live music played in the background as neighbors exchanged news and gossip. Who had fallen ill or on hard times? Who was in good health and prosperous? Who was courting whom?

Some already assembled sections of the frame, called bents, would have lain on the ground. Raising entailed pushing them up and connecting them with horizontal girts until the pieces resembled the outline of a house. The head carpenter gave the signal, and a line of men and women gathered next to the heavy beams. Squatting down, carpenters and townspeople deadlifted the first bent, grunting side by side, pushing upward, and extending their arms until they could go no further. "Lift till the sparks fly out of your eyes; it must go up; if it comes back, it will kill the whole of us," wrote Elijah Kellogg in *The Boy Farmers of Elm Island*, published in 1869, of a raising. A second group came in with pike poles—long, iron-tipped wooden stakes—to push the rising bents further skyward. By tradition, a pine bough then capped the highest point on the ridge to bring good fortune.

Builders erected the frame in a predetermined sequence:

each section cut, assembled, raised, and joined. But in the corner resides a frame's most elaborate joinery. Four individual components intersect here: post, tie beam, wall plate, and rafter. In the kitchen, an intact corner offered me a better understanding of how the rotted-away framing should have appeared. The corner post, cut thicker at the top, tapered slightly toward the bottom, like the gunstock of a rifle pointing downward. That extra thickness accommodated the convergence of the four beams. The tie beam, running parallel with the house's gable end, and the wall plate, running parallel to the eve end, sat atop the post. From the ridgeline of the roof, the rafter descended and rested on both. Mortise-and-tenon joined all of it. This complicated framing gave structural integrity to the building. In the kitchen corner, hidden under paneling, the entire joint was gone, every last piece of it.

The gaping hole rattled my confidence. Replacing rotten timbers meant that I would need to understand the basics of the process, but the repair came with its own challenges that meant more than just pushing beams into place. It demanded raising parts of the frame bearing the weight of the beams above it. Beyond that, the rot proved unpredictable. Some beams had rotted only at the ends, each of those requiring its own sequence of customized patching to fit properly back into place. In the spirit of Richard Macy, I could do the work alone, but it would be easier if I, like the original woodworkers, had some help.

I had studied examples of early American timber framing, but understanding how to rebuild parts of one myself required watching one go up. It was time to find some modern timber framers to see whether they'd be willing to talk. But where to find them?

As a kid, I'd visited Plimoth Patuxet, a living-history museum recreating the Plymouth settlement, established in 1620 by English colonists known as the Pilgrims, along with the Patuxet people on whose land the Pilgrims settled. A vague memory of reproduction houses built there in a colonial style floated through my mind. Just fourteen miles away, it seemed like the best place to start.

Living-history museums occupy a curious place in American life. As educational centers and tourist attractions, they attract school field trips, history buffs, and family vacationers. These groups mingle as costumed interpreters wander around them. The museum, situated near the original Pilgrim and Patuxet settlement, stands on thirty acres of land, a little utopia removed from the surrounding suburbs. One weekend, Liz and I drove down and made our way to the village, which sits on a hillside that stretches to the edge of Plymouth Bay. Down a wide dirt path stood two symmetrical rows of reproduction Pilgrim homes swarming with interpreters going about a typical seventeenth-century day, as if time had stopped in the 1620s.

My eyes pored over the framing of each building, analyzing the joinery. I snapped pictures to study later. The interpreters' answers to my questions about the buildings proved fruitless, though. As *Mayflower* "passengers," they all had specific roles to play, and no one broke character.

They recited facts about their assigned characters or daily life in the colony. Most knew nothing about how the houses had been built. Then a young woman wearing a brown linen dress and felt hat pulled me aside. She glanced over her shoulder, her eyes shifting back and forth. Leaning in, she said in a hushed voice, "The person you need to talk to is Michael Burrey. He built a lot of the houses here and knows *everything* about them." Burrey no longer worked there, but she had his number.

When I called, a faint voice answered the line: "This is Michael."

"My name is Lee McColgan," I said. "I got your number from—" I paused, realizing that I didn't know the woman's name and could describe her only as a "passenger" on the *Mayflower*. "—um, Plimoth Patuxet."

There was silence on the other end of the line.

Awkwardly I rambled on, explaining that I was trying to repair a rotten frame in an eighteenth century house using only period tools and techniques. "Can you help?"

He could. Burrey assured me that he had seen and fixed worse, but short on time, he couldn't come look at it anytime soon. During the school year, he taught preservation carpentry at the North Bennett Street School in Boston, the country's oldest trade school. In the summer, he took on side projects. One of them involved restoring a historic sawmill on the South Shore, just minutes from the Loring House. He suggested that I visit him there.

Down a winding string of back roads, the drive ended

at an overgrown dirt path. As I was wondering whether the GPS directions had failed me, the old mill and a handful of cars came into view. Bustling with activity, groups of students had engrossed themselves in various stages of the restoration. Some looked up from their work and stared at me blankly. They acknowledged my presence but didn't bother with introductions.

In the center of the chaos stood Burrey, a tall, middled-aged man with a calm demeanor and the lean build of a seasoned mountaineer. Bald with a C-ring of short hair around his head, he wore unassuming glasses and the kind of short-sleeved collared shirt NASA engineers wore in the 1960s. A childlike grin stretched across his face as I introduced myself.

"Tell me more about your project," he said softly.

"Well, the frame is in pretty bad shape," I replied. "I dunno if it's worth fixing or if I should tear it down and just rebuild the whole thing."

A look of concern came over his face. "You should be able to save it."

He walked me around the mill, pointing out beams patched with new pieces of wood, his eyes shining with dreamy enthusiasm at the possibilities for fixing my frame. The intermittent sound of power tools made it hard to hear everything he said. "I want to take some pictures," I said, reaching for my pocket but realizing I'd left my phone in the car. "Hang on," I shouted over the noise, dashing back to my car to grab my phone from the console.

The truck parked next to me had drawn little attention at first. But now the logo on its door caught my eye: MLB Restorations. It was Burrey's truck. But instead of a painted logo, the name of the company appeared in black marker on a piece of paper adhered to the vehicle with blue painters tape. It looked like a kindergartner had scribbled a classroom assignment and stuck it on the truck. *Is this guy some kind of mad genius?* I wondered.

Burrey's father had worked as an architect, so he had grown up around blueprints, compasses, drafting tables, and other tools that turn imagination into reality. As a child, he spent lots of time at construction sites, watching structures rise from the ground as cleared patches of land grew into buildings of steel and wood. He absorbed as much as he could retain. Later, with family encouragement, he began to build on his own.

At age thirteen, a visit to the National Gallery of Art in Washington, DC, changed the course of Burrey's life. After touring the exhibits, he wandered into the gift shop and flipped through a copy of *American Barns and Covered Bridges* by Eric Sloane, an author and illustrator who had written a series of books on folk culture in New England. "The book spoke to me so deeply," Burrey said. "I asked my parents to buy it for me."

That book shifted Burrey's attention and focus from modern-day construction to traditional methods. He built reproductions of early American frames, then, moving backward in time, medieval English architecture. "1150 to the seventeenth century, that was timber framing's heyday," he said nostalgically, as if he had lived then. "The designs, the carvings, the geometry—it was the zenith."

Burrey seemed born in the wrong century, cursed to lament the shortcomings of modern society and its builders who live by the mantra of cheaper and faster. "New and improved: new design to improve the bottom line," he said, referring to poor-quality new tools advertised for "innovative" features that fell short of his expectations. As he showed me around the mill, he mentioned that he normally hired a summer apprentice but hadn't found one yet.

"Why don't I come work for you?" I offered. It was a paying gig, albeit not much.

He said yes.

IN COLONIAL New England, an apprenticeship usually lasted seven years. In one contract between Job Lane, a master carpenter in Malden, Massachusetts, and John Queire, his apprentice, the latter agreed to "serve faithfully, not to haunt the taverns, ale houses or places of gaming, nor further commit fornication, or contract matrimony within the said term." My apprenticeship thankfully came with different terms.

Burrey situated his workshop at his house, an antique surrounded by architectural salvage in every direction. Stacks of wood and piles of bricks stood next to rows of doors and windows. Entire frames of old houses lay on the ground or leaned against other structures. The salvaged material had overtaken the property like tangled weeds in a neglected garden. But each piece had potential. A dumpster was out of the question.

With boots in hand, he emerged from the house and sat in a chair by the door, lacing them with the grace of a tailor threading a needle. He motioned to the workshop, an outbuilding behind the house, and set off, my shadow trailing him. Like the yard, the workshop contained a meticulous mess. Neatly sorted piles spilled into every conceivable space. We followed a narrow path—the only way to get from one end of the shop to the other—passing equipment stations, old hand tools, and scraps of wood stacked to the ceiling on all sides. At the center, supported by two sawhorses, lay a large beam marked with small rectangles indicating mortise and tenon joints. It was part of the frame for a reproduction of the 1599 Globe Theater that he was building for a local Shakespearean acting company, in line with his love of Elizabethan-era timber frames.

Brandishing a huge power drill with a corkscrew bit, Burrey drilled a series of adjoining holes. After he hollowed out the small rectangle, he handed me the tool, which pulled at my wrist as I struggled not to drop it. I attempted to copy what he had done, positioning the bit in the center of the lines and squeezing the trigger. The torque jolted through my arm, and the drill felt like it might lift me off the ground and spin my entire body in circles. The auger burrowed its hole. A steady stream of flat, disk-shaped

Using Burrey's oversize mallet and chisel made me feel like Thor. PHOTO BY LIZ BAILEY.

shavings churned up and poured over the beam, falling in little piles at my feet.

The marking for the mortise pocket was rectangular, but the auger bit was round, so it left extra material behind. Burrey handed me a mallet and chisel, also oversized, to excise the excess. Holding the mallet made me feel like Thor. Made to absorb the force of repeated blows, the handle of the chisel was so large that my fingers barely wrapped around it. Its wood had a slight sheen, burnished from decades of use, and the silvery patina of the iron part gleamed. The mallet and chisel dutifully cleaned the wall of the mortise. Slices of wood fiber curled over the beveled edge like potato peels. Every so often, a pause to clear the accumulated shavings from the recess gave my hands a needed break.

At the other end of the beam, Burrey had drawn an outline for the tenon. He handed me a saw, then stood back and watched my cuts: push, pull, repeat. The saw sang in the narrow kerf: *zzz, zah, zzz, zah*. Sawdust drifted to the ground like snow. The saw followed his lines until a small block clapped on the floor. Repeating the process on the opposite side produced the tenon, the plug to fit into the socket. With a hand plane, he cleaned the saw marks, wielding the tool with tremendous control, his neat passes gliding over the rough surface, leaving smooth wood in the tool's wake.

A summer of this, and I should be ready for the Loring House, I thought.

Though time-consuming and exhausting, working with hand tools afforded more control than power tools ever could. Hand tools also proved a lot safer. Cutting myself on a chisel wouldn't mean losing a finger. Efficient designs with no bells and whistles meant not needing to consult a complicated instruction manual. A dozen hand tools, all relatively quiet, could construct an entire timber frame the old-fashioned way. The repetitive tapping of the mallet or the hum of the saw made it easy to get lost in the work, a kind of meditation. The hours slipped away.

But traditional framing did come with a major hurdle: irregular timber. Hewing logs square by hand shaped no two exactly alike. With machined lumber, each piece is the same, interchangeable, like car parts. Mixing parts of a traditional timber frame would have been like putting a Toyota motor into a Ford. Sure, the engines looked similar, but the bolt holes don't align.

"There are two ways to deal with the issue," Burrey had told me. The first was to study each beam and envision a perfect, smaller beam within it, the way Michelangelo looked at a block of marble and saw his vision of David trapped inside. But instead of cutting the entire beam to size, we had to notch out only a small section, or shoulder, where the joint connects. This time-saving method is called square-rule timber framing.

The second approach, scribe-rule timber framing, entailed custom-fitting each joint by laying out all the pieces and making continuous adjustments until everything fit, like a tailor shearing fabric for a bespoke suit. Burrey was using this method for the frame we were cutting. We marked the two connecting pieces of the joints with a Roman numeral, more common in the colonial period than now, to ensure that, when the pile of lumber moved to the site, we knew how to put it together.

The timber was so long that we couldn't maneuver it out the door, so we had to slide it through an open window before loading the beam on a rusty trailer parked in the yard. Together, we heaved it atop a stack of beams already on the trailer. When the last framing crowned the stack, well above my head, we slung straps over each end and fastened them tightly for the drive to western Massachusetts. We called it a day to rest up for the trip the next morning.

Just as the sun was rising, Burrey emerged from the house. We made a checklist of everything we needed, our morning routine, then climbed into his truck for the three-hour drive to the site. We weaved through several small backroads and pulled onto the highway, both of us eyeing the side mirrors to make sure nothing was coming loose. The stack of timbers jostled, settling into place as the trailer rattled down the road. For the first ten minutes, everything went smoothly.

Then a sign indicated roadwork ahead. Smooth pavement gave way to a torn stretch, creating a dip in the road. The truck went over it without problem, but as the trailer followed, we heard a loud snap, and a cloud of gray smoke billowed behind us. "Pull over!" I shouted as Burrey steered to grass on the shoulder. We both jumped out and raced to the trailer. The wheels had buckled under the wheel well, and one of the tires was on fire. Under the weight of the timbers, the rusty axle had broken, and the tire ground into the metal frame, creating so much friction that it went up in a blaze. We kicked sand and gravel onto the flames until it went out.

Burrey had a special way of getting himself into awkward predicaments, then finding a way back out of them. No obstacle loomed too big for him, and he seemed to revel in the chaos of overcoming challenges with the odds against him. He rented a new trailer, and under the baking sun with cars whipping by, we transferred the beams. We drove his disabled trailer back to the house and hit the road again a few hours after breaking down. A scraggly crew of framers met us and, over several days, pushed the frame into place, awing the acting company.

The apprenticeship with Burrey called for lots of grunt work in exchange for tidbits of knowledge. After morning checklists, he let intuition guide our days and planned little, a sharp contrast to my former finance colleagues, some of whom planned the entire year in advance. Some days, he and I milled and stacked boards; other days, I cleaned the shop—all worth it for a brief lesson on how to sharpen a tool, cut a tenon, or use a hand plane. I also learned why the logo on his truck was scribbled in marker and taped to the door. He was indeed a mad genius, but he had a practical reason for it. His truck had commercial plates, and state law required the vehicle to display a company logo. Eventually he had one painted on the truck, but during my time working with him, he hadn't gotten to it yet. As summer ended, so did the apprenticeship, so it was time to get back to working on the Loring House. First order of business: finding the right lumber.

As the sunny afternoons grew shorter day by day, Bryson, my old black lab, and I made a habit of walking from the pasture to the forest. We headed out, Bryson trailing behind me, stopping to sniff, losing himself in a patch of grass. When he looked up, seeing that I had ranged ahead, he trotted toward me, his back leg stiff as wood, until he reached me and stopped, teetering for a moment. We continued to a blue gate at the woods' edge. He stared at me until I opened it, and we made our way down a long path surrounded by thick brush and trees. In 1702, when the Loring House was built, workmen had cleared the land for livestock to graze. Now only a rolling fence of tossed stones remained from that time.

Civilization receded from sight. Trees towered above us. Some grew straight, while others, coiling through the air, looked like ivy on the side of a building. All stretched their canopy branches wide. Giants, they swayed in the breeze as Bryson and I inhaled the fresh air. Then a thought occurred to me: *I could use trees on the property to reframe the house.*

But harvesting these complex organisms posed a moral dilemma that I hadn't considered until reading *The Hidden Life of Trees* by Peter Wohlleben. Trees, like people, form friendships. Some care for others by providing nutrients through their root systems. Wohlleben tells of coming across the stump of a tree felled 400 years earlier but still alive because surrounding trees kept pumping nutrients to it. Trees are more like us than I had realized.

My forest showed similar evidence of these friendships. The large eastern white pines grew evenly spaced apart, their canopy branches tactfully allowing neighbors to share the sunlight. Trees of the same species respected one another and for good reason. One tree alone in a field stands at the mercy of the elements. A forest, however, can regulate the climate, the community creating an ecosystem that modulates extremes of heat and cold, stores water, and generates humidity when needed. Because trees react to dramatic change so slowly (compared to humans), maintaining a steady ecosystem offers them an evolutionary benefit. It's in their best interest to work together.

Wohlleben's book also taught me that trees can talk, using a language of scent. If a predator is attacking—an insect or mammal chewing on leaves, for example—a tree will emit gases that forewarn its neighbors. They can tell time as well, dropping their leaves before winter and budding as spring returns.

But beyond the moral issue stood another, more practical consideration. Freshly felled trees, known as green wood, contain more water, making the wood softer and easier to cut with hand tools in the same way that it's easier to cut into a juicy filet mignon than into overcooked shoe leather. "The water molecules interact with hydroxyl groups on cellulose molecules and effectively weaken the chemical bond between the wood cells," scientist Jeff Langlois told me. As a bonus, freshly cut trees also produce pleasing smells, such as mint from fresh birch, butterscotch from some species of pine, and hints of apple cider from the tannic acids in oak. Kiln-dried lumber and composites glued together with noxious adhesives don't smell anywhere near as nice.

I had worked with green wood before. In the Vermont of my childhood, the hikes behind Bobby Newbury's house evolved into campouts at a mountainside site with a scenic overlook. We simply called the granite outcropping The Rock. Recruiting a few more kids from school, we formed a small band, regularly trudging up to the spot. One summer Saturday, we bivouacked, and a can of beef stew scavenged from my parents' pantry served as dinner. But no one remembered to bring utensils.

"Why don't we make them?" someone suggested.

Near the campsite grew a patch of striped maple saplings, which we cut with the folding saw of a Swiss Army knife. The moist sawdust clogged its sharp teeth, but the fresh bark separated easily. The underlying cambium felt slimy like a frog. Whittling the wood sliced away fibers that peeled off in long strips. Our finished spoons looked more like spatulas, each of the bowls lopsided and shallow, but they worked. In the firelight that flickered across our soot-covered faces, we shared the simple indulgence of the stew. Working freshly cut wood then held little complication or consequence for me.

But cutting massive beams for a house differed a great

deal from making a spoon. As green wood dries, it shrinks, its movement unpredictable. The more moisture in the wood, the greater the chances that it will move. The longer the piece of wood, the more dramatic that movement can be. Selecting trees that had grown straight up could save a lot of headaches, sure, but even that strategy offered no guarantee that they'd remain straight after drying out. Some trees with straight trunks leaned, growing on a hillside, for example. Some appeared straight but had subtle twists, sometimes difficult to see, hidden in the pattern of the bark. These differences resulted from decisions the trees themselves made. In a forest, every young tree waits for an older tree to fall, creating a canopy opening. Some gnarl themselves chasing sunlight. Sometimes the tactic works, but it can prove detrimental. A slope too steep can make a tree unstable enough that a strong wind could knock it down. Trees can overcompensate for this lack of equilibrium by building excessive layers on the sloping side, which requires more support. That effort to fight gravity creates a buildup of tension or compression, known as reaction wood, that causes problems for woodworkers. The stresses lie dormant until you are processing the wood for building. Tension and compression also affect movement as wood dries.

"One night, I heard what sounded like a gunshot coming from the cellar," wrote Bruce Hoadley of living in a timber-framed house in. "Racing down the stairs, I found nothing alarming. Looking up, I discovered the source of the noise. The lower face of one of the hemlock joists had a gaping cross-break. The dryness of the furnace heat was the final increment of unbearable shrinkage tension, causing the beam to fail abruptly."

RETURNING TO the forest, Bryson and I hunted for white oak, the predominant kind used in the Loring House frame. This time, he took the lead and I lagged behind, a field guide of eastern species in hand to help me identify bark and leaf shapes. Whenever I lagged too far behind, he waited for me, our roles reversed. A good boy, he never strayed far.

Some barks felt rough and scaled like a reptile, while others felt smoother, with thin creases like elephant hide. Some trees had fallen long ago, no more than partial trunks left standing. The ruined stumps stood like chimney stacks after a house burns to the ground. The rest of the trees, speckled with white fungi, were decomposing into the soil. The exposed cambium revealed countless holes from insects and woodpeckers.

White oak, a slow-growing tree, produces dense wood impervious to rot. In its bark and leaves, it contains lots of tannic acid, a bitter toxin that makes the tree unpalatable to chewing insects. But its resistance to rot comes primarily from cell growths called tyloses that act as defenders. When stressed by drought or infection, tyloses dam the cells to prevent further damage. This botanical defense matters to woodworkers because white oak is porous. If not for tyloses, those pores would soak up water, creating an environment ideal for microorganisms to consume the wood. Tyloses function in the same way that a thick coat of varnish seals the wood on the surface of a bar, repelling the spills of busy bartenders or tipsy drinkers.

Bryson and I could find only a handful of white oak, all saplings, so we turned back toward the house. His pace slowed, eyes drooping, breathing heavy, a slight wheeze when he exhaled. From a red bucket left for the horses, he lapped water, then lay on the grass.

I called Burrey. "Where can I find white oak for timber framing?" He recommended a local sawmill, a departure from walking in the footsteps of Richard Macy. If Macy needed lumber, he felled it himself. In my case, a phone call placed an order as if for pizza, and a few weeks later a flat-bed unloaded the timber in my driveway. Part of me felt that Macy would have disapproved.

Sawn into square beams, the milled lumber had curved lines on its surfaces, marks from the large circular saw that ripped through the sapwood, shaving off long strips of bark. The repair pieces needed to match the existing frame, so the mill cut them a few inches wider in order for me to finish them by hand. Burrey didn't teach me how to do that, so the illustrations from *A Museum of Early American Tools* by Eric Sloane showed me how.

When the Loring House went up, hewing took place in two stages. First, the carpenter stood atop the log and, with a felling axe, cut a series of notches, each a foot apart, across the entire length. Then he climbed down and, with a broad axe, cut off the sections between the notches. Severing the cellulose fibers, the notches allowed him to chop off large chunks whole. When he had flattened the entire side, he rotated the log and repeated the process on the remaining three sides.

In books, illustrations of carpenters balancing on logs while clutching razor-sharp tools looked intimidating, but I had to try. I dragged the beam to a quiet corner of the yard at the woods' edge. The sound of passing cars came only as a whisper. Here, groomed landscape, curated with industrial mowers, trimmers, and weed whackers, met the untamed wild. On one side, the pasture unfurled toward the sun shining over the horizon. On the other, the land sloped into the forest before dropping into a shallow ravine. A marshy basin collected rainwater that drained from the hillside. There, low-growing wetland plants thrived, their bright greens radiant as neon signs. In the distance, the forest's edge appeared opaque, the jagged canopy cutting into the clouds. But up close, I could look through the dense thicket of greens, browns, and purples as if peering behind a curtain.

Pulling and rolling, I situated the beam on a flat patch suitable for the work. *Bend with your knees*, said a voice in my head as I squatted. Lifting it, I propped the beam on two smaller timbers to keep the hewing axe from hitting the rocky soil and chipping the blade. The axe emerged from its leather sheath, and my feet wobbled on the narrow beam. Foraging nearby, a curious squirrel stopped, sat on its haunches, then darted away, its fluffy tail fluttering behind it.

The first cut needed to land directly between my feet.

Nervously I studied the target, imagining the axe missing its mark and slicing off a toe, forcing me to crawl through the grass to find the bloody digit. A bead of sweat ran down my forehead, stinging my eye. My hands felt clammy. "I have to commit," I said aloud. "No hesitation."

The axe rose slowly until it hung suspended overhead. All my might brought the blade down like a medieval executioner chopping off a head. The blade skipped off the hard oak, the handle almost flying from my hands, and the beam shook. A loud knock echoed off trees in the distance. A deep breath, and the axe rose again. The second time, it struck cleanly, lodging into the fibers. All toes intact. From several more cuts, a small wedge emerged.

As I worked my way down the beam, trying to keep my balance, aided by the traction from the rubber soles of my boots, I thought about Thomas Macy performing the same task while wearing flat-soled leather shoes. That thought gave me an even greater appreciation for what he and the other workmen of his time had done. From the ravine, a breeze swept over me, cooling the sweat seeping from every pore. My breath came heavy. It took the better part of an hour to cut all the required notches. After stepping back down, the ground felt firmer than it had before I started.

Burrey had lent me a broad axe. From the blunt end, called the poll, the head of the tool flared into a round, flat mass of iron that ended at the edge of the blade. It resembled a flounder cut clean down the middle, one half discarded. The iron looked rusty brown except for the glistening steel of the freshly sharpened blade. The coffee-colored handle, shorter than that of the felling axe, had a kink in it, kicked out to one side. My hands gripped it like a baseball bat. The first swing quickly made clear why the handle had the funny shape. Cutting along the beam, my knuckles would have caught the hardwood on the downstroke of the cut. The bend in the handle kept my hands away from the rough timber. With a few swings, the foot-long sections popped off, flying through the air like grasshoppers in an open field. A tiny nick in the blade left a small track in its wake.

With each swing, the mechanics of my clunky handling of the axe improved. The steel sliced deep into the stringy fibers of a once-living organism, hacking at its carcass. The task required tremendous focus. As I wielded the tool, all my muscles tensed in a violent exertion of force that somehow also felt strangely peaceful. Lulled by repetition, my mind wandered, thinking but not thinking. The moment contained no worry about all the obstacles that lay ahead. It consisted solely of the wood, the axe, and me as the sun sank slowly in the sky. By dusk, the beam lay square.

Later, a simple handsaw allowed me to cut tenons into it, modeled on the intricate joinery of the three corner posts that remained in the house. I hewed the beam and cut the joinery myself, but raising and fitting the repair pieces required more hands. My apprenticeship with Burrey entailed working on a handful of projects with other students. "Interested in some timber-framing repair at my house on the South Shore? Paid work," I texted a handful of them. Replies came from Ian Cubie and Aaron Troyan-sky, talented craftsmen who had completed the preservation carpentry program.

On a Saturday morning, an old Subaru pulled into the driveway and parked by the barn. Lanky, with short messy hair and plain glasses, Cubie greeted me with a smile, his head tilting to one side. His clothes consisted of natural materials: canvas and linen fabrics, boots made of leather, all of it in earthy browns, greens, and tans. It looked like he had grown from the forest behind the house. Before we had time to exchange pleasantries, another car arrived. Troyansky, also tall and thin, joined us. Together, we looked like brothers. Stranger still, we all looked like younger versions of Burrey. The guys unloaded their tools, still clean and shiny, and we headed into the house to examine the rotten frame.

"The first thing we need to do is bring the post inside," I said.

The protruding tenons gave us purchase for gripping the heavy beam. The freshly cut wood felt damp, the tree's cells still swollen with water. Cubie took one end, I took the other, and Troyansky held the middle. We heaved the beam inside, stumbling over our own feet while struggling to move the dead weight, as if we were moving a body, then lowered it carefully to the floor.

"We're going to need better access to the underlying sill," Cubie observed.

I nodded, my crowbar prying at one of the floorboards

near the new post's spot, nails squealing as they emerged from dense, dried oak. Exposed, the sill sat on a loosely laid row of flat stones abutted by a dirt floor dotted with the occasional animal bone or shard of pottery. The familiar musty smell of the basement wafted upward. A finished space, the kitchen had walls covered in paneling, windows and doors adorned with painted moldings. But in the corner, we had torn it open, ripping away the flesh and baring its bones.

"I'll start here," I said, pointing to one end of the beam, "and push it up into place."

"We'll have to make sure the tenon on the bottom lines up," Cubie added as he positioned himself on the other end.

As I squatted, my hands cupped the wood. "On three . . . one . . . *two* . . ."

Aaron joined me, and in one motion we all heaved, pushing the beam like the soldiers raising the flag at Iwo Jima. The beam stood upright, and we huddled around it, holding it in place, trying not to step on one another's toes. From a nearby pile, Cubie grabbed a piece of two-by-four and used it as a brace, tacking one end to the post and the other to the sill until the post stood on its own.

We were replacing the entire corner post, but the beams connecting to it had rotted only at their ends. We could repair these sections of frame with scarf joints: patching new wood where the damage had occurred, allowing us to salvage most of the original beams. We had to make three separate repair pieces, each about four feet long, and lower the pieces onto the post into matching joinery that overlapped, tying the ends together like the fingers of two clasped hands. But planks nailed to the rafters stood in the way.

"Maybe we should cut a hole in the roof?" Cubie offered. Troyansky agreed. Studying the corner, I hoped for another option but couldn't see one. They were right.

Troyansky climbed a folding aluminum ladder and peeled shingles from the roof with a crowbar. Crumbling bits of tar tumbled onto the deck. To speed some processes, we conceded to using power tools, so Cubie ran a long orange extension cord through a kitchen window, plugged a circular saw into it, and raised it to the roof. The tool roared to life. Drowning the hum of the electric motor, the saw's teeth ripped across the planks, leaving a clean cut behind. The two men removed the boards, opening a gaping hole. Natural light poured into the house. Through the ceiling, wispy streaks of white clouds floated lazily on a current of air, the blue sky framed by old dark wood.

Then Liz came home. "How long is the kitchen going to be a construction site?" she asked, alarmed. I didn't have a good answer.

Cubie, Troyansky, and I moved outside, to the deck, where we determined who would handle which repair. We each retrieved our chisels. Mine emerged from an open wooden toolbox with a long dowel handle. Ian and Aaron kept theirs in wooden boxes with sliding lids, which they had made at North Bennett Street. Their mallets had metal heads with rolled strips of rawhide on the faces that added

To repair the rotten framing,
we had to cut a hole in the roof.
Photo by Liz Bailey.

Cutting the joinery on the repair pieces turned out to be the easy part. PHOTO BY LIZ BAILEY.

weight but still provided cushioning to prevent marring their chisel handles.

With my antique carpenter's square on one side of the beam, my weight shifted from feet to index finger and thumb, spread wide for stability, as the awl scribed the line. The pointed end of the tool ran along the straight metal edge of the L-shaped ruler with a rich brown patina and the slight imperfection of hand-punched numerals, scratching a mark visible against the grain. We all immersed ourselves in the work. After cutting the joinery, I chiseled the wood free-hand. Cubie and Troyansky sawed and chiseled away without distraction. Amid the whacking of mallets and panel saws gouging narrow kerfs in the wood, an hour passed without any of us saying a word.

Cutting the joinery on the repair pieces turned out to be the easy part. Matching it on the beams fixed to the rest of the house and suspended overhead on temporary braces proved far more difficult. The tie beam tottered as I cut it from the underside, arching backward and sawing upside-down. Moving to the top of the beam required working from a ladder, my head poking through the fresh hole in the roof. More than 300 years of subsidence had caused just about every part of the structure to fall out of square. In some places, the foundation consisted of a layer of field stone that sat above the frost line, so centuries of freezing and thawing had shifted the frame at random. Parts of the house sank deep into the soft earth, while others remained on high ground. As a result, some beams slanted like seesaws. We worked among trapezoids, existing in a land unsquared.

Aligning the pieces also proved difficult, and we had to test-fit each one. If a joint was too tight, a few mallet blows either aligned it perfectly or wedged it so firmly that we struggled to remove it for more finishing. I trimmed a little here or there, scribing lines to custom-fit each individual joint, and tried again. After multiple attempts, the piece finally fit, connecting like a Lego block snapping in place. A large drill with a foot-long auger bit bored four holes for pegs to hold it all in place. A rawhide mallet drove the first tapered peg into its destination. Each strike created more resistance, the peg widening the deeper it went, tightening against the hole. Cubie and Troyansky followed suit, driving in more pegs until every piece had fallen into place.

We had paid close, methodical attention to every detail of the repair, analyzing and overanalyzing each step. But we put the room back in order with more haste, scrambling to seal the roof and refinish the walls. "I'll deal with that later," I said, declaring the job done for now.

Three months had passed since discovering the rotten corner, leaving fifteen to get the house ready. We assembled in the kitchen to celebrate. From the outset, I wanted the house to serve as a gathering place, and it had brought together our small group of carpenters. The restoration was no longer a solitary pursuit. We joked and laughed, recapping the day, sharing stories from our experience as timber framers. We felt like kids again, building shelters in the

The repaired corner of the timber frame.

Ian Cubie, I, and Aaron Troyansky looked like younger versions of Burrey. PHOTO BY LIZ BAILEY.

woods with friends. We all smiled as Liz took a photo to capture the moment. Hovering above us, the freshly cut tan patches of the newly repaired frame contrasted sharply with the earthy brown, oxidized timber cut centuries earlier. We looked happy, and from the photo, an entirely different version of myself stared back at me. A wild mop of hair and a stubbly beard had overtaken my face. Dirt covered me from head to toe.

I went to the bathroom to wash up, the grime on my hands coming off with a withered bar of soap, the water turning brown before draining down the sink. When my hands were clean, I splashed water on my face and leaned into the mirror, tilting my head to one side, then the other to make sure I hadn't missed any patches. With my head close to the glass, more of the room behind me was reflected in it. On the ceiling, near the shower, a large black spot had appeared, something I hadn't seen before.

What the hell is that?

III.

The Lime Cycle

I take pride in this great wall, and plaster it
with dust and sand lest a least hole should be
left in this name; and for all the care I take
I lose sight of my true being.

—*Rabindranath Tagore*

SEASONED FOR SEVERAL YEARS, A STACKED PILE of firewood stood against the back wall of the garage, a small outbuilding constructed in the 1950s. The season's first chill ushered me to gather an armful of logs and fallen branches snapped into kindling. The bundle then made its way to the brick hearth in the main hall, one of the house's seven fireplaces. Prying open the cast iron damper, installed after the chimney had been built, released bits of black soot that rained on me. Several crumpled pages of an old newspaper formed the fire's base, followed by twigs in a small conical pile. Surrounded by the sharp smell of sulfur, the flame of a struck match touched the corner of one of the pages, igniting it. Black smoke rose through the flue and vanished into the crisp night air.

When the twigs had reduced to embers, a few logs joined the conflagration. Engulfed, they blackened and burned. From a kitchen cupboard came a slender green bottle of Scotch. The cork stopper twisted with a faint squeak, and the bottle opened with a *thoomp*. Pouring a glass, I sank into my red wingback chair near the fireplace. The whisky swirled in the glass, amber liquid legging the sides before spinning back to the bottom. The fire warmed my own legs until my pants grew too hot to touch.

With more wood, the flames grew taller, throwing shadows across the room. The pyre of logs crackled. Occasionally a glowing ember popped from the hearth and shot onto the rug, forcing me to spring from my chair to stamp it out. The playful, flickering light skipped off every jut and recess of the plaster, its subtle texture produced by hand. In the summer months, the room looked dark, the low ceilings making it feel like a cave, but the shadows jumping and twirling around me made it come alive, resurrected. The old plaster, I decided, was worth saving.

AT FIRST, the black spot on the bathroom ceiling looked like a bug, but it didn't move. As I approached, it remained motionless. Bracing myself against the wall, I stood on tip toe for a closer look. Tiny black polka dots blotted the wider surface. Before we bought it, a thorough walkthrough of the house hadn't revealed any black spots. Where had they come from?

My red wingback chair.
PHOTO BY ARI KELLERMAN.

Before putting it on the market, Lydia Hale's family had the house cleaned thoroughly. Then it sat, unoccupied, for months. Daily showers now filled the bathroom with steam that lingered because no one ever installed a fan in the room. Countless thirsty microscopic organisms, lying dormant, suddenly began to flourish, colonizing the ceiling. It all added up to a mold problem.

During one of the remodeling jobs, contractors had removed the original lime plaster ceiling in the bathroom, replacing it with modern drywall board. The new material had a hard finish, like the glaze on porcelain. But the recurring changes in humidity caused the drywall to expand and contract, creating small fractures in the brittle coating, imbuing it with crackle, the surface fractures of glazed ceramics. Those tiny cracks were trapping moisture in which mold was growing.

The drywall needed to come down. Demolition didn't pose any problems, but restoring the original ceiling required more consideration. I wanted to reproduce the rich, textured surface of the original plasterwork, but how?

During my apprenticeship with Burrey, he told me stories of an individual I'll call Olivia Morland, a traditional plasterer with whom he had worked for many years. In additional to making repairs, she reproduced ornamental plasterwork, casting elaborate designs in molds and adhering them to walls and ceilings. Burrey's shop also contained examples of her decorative painting. In a corner stood two large wooden columns that she masterfully had painted to resemble marble. Maybe she could help me. She lived on Nantucket, where Richard Macy also had made his home, thirty miles south of Cape Cod. It felt like the universe was pulling me out to sea, a piece of driftwood bobbing on the tide.

On the phone, Morland told me that she had spent the last few years restoring one of the island's nineteenth century houses simply called "86 Main." She needed more workers to finish the job and seemed to care only about how soon I could get there. Reaching the island required taking the ferry across Nantucket Sound. She told me to book the early boat but not what kind of work I'd be doing or what to bring. A man named Colin would pick me up at the dock. I booked my ticket, two weeks in advance, and waited.

LIZ AND I had honeymooned on Nantucket. For that trip, we booked a mid-morning ticket, which allowed us to sleep in and take our time driving to the dock. We stopped for coffee and greasy breakfast sandwiches, splurging for a parking spot next to the boat. We arrived around 10 a.m., strolled aboard, roller bags in tow, without having to wait in line, and sat by a window.

The ship's idling engine murmured as we waited to depart. No other passengers sat near us, so it felt like we had the boat to ourselves. Across the aisle sat a man wearing a polo shirt and pressed, salmon-colored pants dotted with embroidered whales. His index finger flicked the screen of his tablet, scrolling through brightly colored charts. His crossed legs had raised the hem of one pant leg, exposing a tan, sockless ankle above a brown loafer. Sitting next to him, a woman clutching a designer leather purse was leaning on his shoulder. A large diamond ring refracted the light hitting her finger and sparkled in the midmorning sun. She looked out the window, her eyes vacant. Somewhere behind us, another woman broke the silence by describing a recent restaurant visit. "You *have* to try the lobster ravioli," she said. "Really, everything there is wonderful." A travel pamphlet from the ticket counter highlighted some of the island's attractions: brewery tour, old mill, basket museum. Across the bay, sequined water shimmered peacefully to an endless horizon.

On the day I went to work for Morland, my alarm sounded at 4 a.m. Foregoing a shower, I dressed in blurry darkness and shuffled to the car. Still groggy after the hour-long drive to Hyannis, I parked in the economy lot and trudged down a long sidewalk beneath the glow of streetlights, following the sound of the ferry's engine and the queasy smell of fuel and fish. A line of passengers waiting to board wrapped around the entire dock. First light was breaking by the time the line started moving. A crew member emerged from the boat, unclipped a guard rope, and collected tickets. By the time I boarded, most of the seats had been occupied, some with passengers, some with a bag or jacket. Nantucket has the country's highest concentration of antebellum houses and some of the nation's most expensive new construction. It needs contractors—and lots of them—but even a good contractor's salary makes it difficult to afford property there, so workers take the ferry every morning.

As I settled into one of the few available seats, we lurched out to sea. The massive vessel bounced over choppy waves. My hands gripped the armrests as acid sloshed in my gut, churning like the water in the boat's wake. My eyes focused on the flat horizon, trying to trick my body into forgetting that it was bobbing up and down. I didn't want to have to dash to the rail of the ship and throw up over the side.

Small bands of workmen in matching shirts—with neon construction yellow a popular color—clustered together. Company logos featuring hammers, wrenches, and concrete mixing trucks hinted at their trades. They wore pants of heavy canvas, some tattered, some covered in paint.

"You see that homah last night?" said one man in a heavy Boston accent.

"Oh yeah," said another.

"Right ovah the wall."

The man sitting next to me had slouched over, trying for another hour of sleep before we docked. The leather on both his work boots had worn away in even circles, exposing shiny steel toes. He smelled like a halved onion left all day in the late summer sun, a trace of alcohol seeping through his skin. He didn't say a word the entire ride.

Unlike my honeymoon, this trip afforded no time to laze on the beach, no fancy restaurants, no riding bikes with little baskets strapped to the handlebars. It was Monday morning, and a week of hard labor awaited. It felt like we were on the boat to Alcatraz.

On the island, the sea air reeked of ocean muck drying in the sun as the tide receded. In a few places, glimmers of the old fishing port lingered, but no freshly caught fish or casks of whale oil lined the docks. Storefronts displayed trinkets, home décor, and designer clothing. The dock bustled with activity. Ferry workers pulled wheeled carts, linked together like railcars, full of checked luggage. A flock of passengers hunted for bags, picking through the carts like seagulls pulling scraps of food from a dumpster. I grabbed a coffee from a nearby shop and waited. At the far end of the dock, a tall man—evenly buzzed hair, black beard, work clothes—appeared, then stood motionless amid the frenzy.

"Colin?" I asked.

He nodded. "Welcome to the island."

We walked across the wharf to a parking lot filled with European sports cars and SUVs, all waxed and buffed, sparkling in the morning light. Colin opened the driver's side door of a gray flatbed truck. It looked like the paint job had been finished with a cheese grater. As I cleared a pile of tools and clothing from the passenger seat, the truck roared to throaty life, sounding as if the muffler had fallen off. The vehicle bumped over the scenic cobbles of Main Street, my coffee sloshing across my lap despite valiant efforts to keep it level.

Vans and other trucks had parked all around a large white

house with black shutters and a cupola on the roof. Workers came and went through the front door, bees swarming a hive. Colin led me down a flight of stairs to the basement, which was teeming with contractors, plumbers, electricians, carpenters, and more, all consumed with myriad tasks. He mouthed something that I couldn't hear over the roar of a power saw shredding lumber.

"*I'll be right back!*" he repeated.

Trying to stay out of the way, I stood frozen. A man in clean clothing approached and mistook me for one of the cleaning crew. He delegated instructions as I looked at him blankly, confused. Before I could choke down my pride and say something, he departed to address some other issue, leaving me unattended once more. Several months earlier, I had worked as a vice president at a large financial firm, but now I had no authority. The career I so carefully had curated and then abandoned never fully felt like a part of me. Now, adrift on an island far offshore, it felt even more remote. But 86 Main didn't offer a sense of belonging, either. To the other workers, I was another outsider. Feeling alone for the first time since entering the trade, I questioned my decision to become a preservationist. What had I done?

After a few minutes, Colin returned, lugging a large white bucket. "You're going to do some pointing."

Repointing masonry consists of chiseling old mortar from the gaps between stones or brick courses, then refilling them with fresh mortar—a good task for a beginner.

He wedged a screwdriver under the bucket lid and worked it around the circumference until the lid popped off. In the bucket, a gelatinous white substance had the consistency of cottage cheese.

"This is lime putty," he said. "Don't get any in your eye. It burns like hell."

His trowel sliced into it, scooping up a brick-sized clump. The material made an unsettling slurping sound, like sucking soup from a spoon. He slung it from the trowel into a second bucket with a *thwap*, added sand, and combined the two with a drill fitted with a long mixer attachment. The two ingredients merged, turning gray and developing the texture of brown sugar. He grabbed a pump sprayer, spritzed the foundation of the building with water, and shaped a handful of mortar into a ball. If the stone in the foundation was too dry, he explained, it would absorb the water in the mortar, which would shrink and crack, hence the sprayer. He sliced off thin lines of the gray material and pressed it into gaps in the foundation, packing the mortar until it oozed through thin openings around the stone.

"That's all there is to it. Good luck," he said and vanished again.

Mimicking Colin, I reached into the bucket and squeezed a handful of cold mortar against my palm. Water seeped from my fingers. The mortar slipped awkwardly off the pointing tool, splattering on the floor. Each time some fell, I glanced over my shoulder, hoping that no one had noticed. I wanted to look like I knew what I was doing.

My technique eventually developed a working rhythm, allowing me, after a few hours, to finish one side of the foundation. Standing back to admire my work, I wiped the sweat from my brow, forgetting that lime still covered my hand. The tiny particles raked across my eyeball and triggered searing pain. My eyelid clamped down, tears streaming down my cheek as I stumbled to the bathroom to rinse it out.

Colin was right. It burned like hell.

Why did anyone still use lime?

TRADITIONAL PLASTER and mortar both contain lime, referring to the limestone from which it comes. Limestone, a sedimentary rock, forms when the skeletal remains of small marine organisms sink to the bottom of the ocean and accrete in layers. On land, it occurs where changing climates have dried out the seabed—turning fertile estuaries into wilting deserts, for example—or where the movement of the earth's crust pushes layers of it to the surface.

When the Loring House was built, quarry workers split small pieces of limestone from glacial boulders or outcrops of exposed bedrock that they could access, move, and process easily with simple tools. A quarryman drilled small holes in the stone, deepening them with a spoon-shaped chisel, and hammered into it a row of wedges that fractured the rock apart. In 1757, naturalist John Bartram described this "plug-and-feather" process in a letter to Jared Elliot.

My method is to bore into rock about 6 inches deep, having drawn a line from one end to the other, in which I bore holes about a foot asunder, more or less, according to the freeness of the rock. . . . All the holes must have their wedges drove together, one after another, gently, that they may strain all alike. You may hear by their ringing when they strain well. Then with the sharp edge of the sledge strike hard on the rock in the line between every wedge, which will crack the rock; then drive the wedges again. It generally opens in a few minutes after the wedges are drove tight.

Without the necessary tools to plug and feather, a quarrier could resort to fire splitting, a crude but effective means of achieving the same end. A fire atop the boulder or bedrock heated the stone before the workman heaved a large blunt object, such as a cannonball, overhead, and dropped it. Repeated blows broke the stone apart.

For the builders of the Loring House, limestone proved scarce. Builders had discovered quarries in Providence, Rhode Island, in 1661 and Newbury, Massachusetts, in 1697, but they were small. Builders alternately could make plaster and mortar with seashells, from which limestone comes in the first place. Mounds of discarded shells, called middens, offered a ready supply for early colonists, who found them in and around the empty settlements of Native Americans who had succumbed to the Great Dying, waves of lethal diseases brought by Europeans that swept through the Western Hemisphere.

When colonists had depleted the middens, they gathered shells from beaches. One 1694 storm littered the coast of Lynn in the Massachusetts Bay Colony with so many shells that it sent the townspeople into a frenzy. "It caused a lime hysteria," according to historian Paul Jenison. The scarcity of shells became such an issue that some local governments stepped in to regulate it. In 1728, the town council of Providence recorded "that the Long oyster bed that hath bin the principal supply of oysters for the inhabitants and poore of our several Neighboring Precincts now likely to be wholey destroyed by those that take and have took up the trade of Lime burning." Anyone caught taking shells for the trade had to pay a fine of forty shillings, about £290 or $360 in today's money.

To make plaster, workers needed to transform the stone or shells into a putty. They fired the raw materials for eighteen hours in a field kiln that reached temperatures from 800 to 1,700 degrees Fahrenheit. The heat burned off the carbon dioxide, leaving a volatile, powdery, white material called quicklime. When quicklime combines with water, in a process called slaking, a chemical reaction occurs. Releasing extreme heat, the slurry hisses and bubbles, steam rising from it as if from a cauldron. At the end of the reaction, a milky, pliable putty results. Mixing that putty with sand and animal hair gives the material structural strength, allowing workers to affix it to walls and ceilings or to fill joints between stone and brick. Exposed to the air, it oxidizes, reabsorbing carbon dioxide and hardening back to stone. The whole process is called the lime cycle.

At the end of my first day pointing, dried spots of white plaster covered my clothing. It looked like someone had rolled me through flour like a piece of chicken before frying. Hunched over a corner of the foundation, my knees and lower back throbbed. Footsteps descended the stairs. Someone stopped behind me.

"How's everything going?" said a woman with a strong English accent.

A short, middle-aged woman, Morland had an athletic build and youthful appearance. She had pulled her dark hair back except for a curtain of bangs that hung above her eyes. She was wearing a navy-blue T-shirt and jeans. Born in the Cotswolds to an artist mother, she had grown up around paint and spent her life working with her hands. She left Britain at age sixteen to travel the world, returning at age twenty-nine to attend the University of Portsmouth. After earning a degree in conservation architecture, she became the first woman accepted into London's Worshipful Company of Plaisterers, a trade guild formed in 1501.

"I left again promptly," she said without elaboration. Untethered, she landed on Nantucket, called here for work, and never left. "Very few people were doing traditional plasterwork in the States. It wasn't like Europe. I saw a need." She gravitated to the vernacular style of building in America—"It's human"—quickly establishing a reputation on the island. Wholly consumed by her work, she doggedly put in long hours with little interest in self-promotion. People came to her, and she answered only to her clients. "I'm feral," she liked to say.

Colin put it a different way: "She's a whirlwind."

In the basement of 86 Main, she examined the results of my efforts. A drop of mortar fell from the pointing tool in my hand and landed on the floor with a splat that felt louder than before, as if amplified by her presence. Working under the careful watch of a Renaissance master must have felt something like this.

She scooped a ball of mortar from the bucket, fishing a slender metal tool from a nearby canvas bag, and filled the narrow gap that I had been following. She packed the opening at twice my pace. Over the course of decades, she had restored miles of stone and brick. Her hands were weathered, the skin rough and split like the old tree branches that washed up on the beach. None of her mortar hit the floor. We worked together as the sun slipped into the ocean. Reds, oranges, yellows, and purples, visible through a tiny window at street level, swirled above the water, the horizon dissolving into darkness. The workday was ending.

I stood, arching my back, and all my joints popped. Outside, the ocean breeze cooled my face, the salt air fresh after a day in a musty basement. Some of the workers headed to a local bar to relax over a few beers, but my body needed sleep. Morland kindly had offered me the guest bedroom in her house, a few blocks away. "Feel free to have anything you like," she said warmly in the kitchen, her cheeks crimping as she smiled. She took a deep breath, then: "I'm headed out." She disappeared through a side door to spend the rest of the evening restoring antiques in a small workshop a few streets over.

My plaster-caked clothing carefully came off without making a total mess on the floor, and a hot shower soothed my tired muscles. But at the sink, nothing happened when I turned the brass faucet handle.

That's strange, I thought, still holding my toothbrush.

Under the sink, the water lines dangled lifeless, not yet connected to the fixture. Dressed, I made my way to the sink in the kitchen, which revealed more unfinished projects: a new gas stove still in the box, electrical switches without covers, wires growing from walls like weeds. The house hung in a perpetual state of renovation. Except for a few shriveled vegetables and some cans of seltzer, the refrigerator sat empty. Morland was working so hard on 86 Main and other projects that she didn't have enough time to take care of herself. My stomach snarled. I found some crackers in a cabinet. Tearing into the package, I devoured them, ravenous.

The next morning, I returned to the basement of 86 Main, self-sufficient this time, and the pointing continued. The morning passed without incident, but a small basement window showed a churning, overcast sky. A storm was coming.

Dark clouds shifted over the spit, bringing unpredictably

heavy rain. With gutters only partially installed, a sheet of water poured over the side of the house. It seeped into the basement, flooding the work area, catching everyone off-guard. The plastic pipe of the basement drain still had extra height to keep the fresh concrete for the new floor from spilling into it. The pipe shot up like a periscope, high above ground level, as water filled the basement. It was coming fast and had to rise a full foot before reaching the drain opening.

"*Cut that fuckin' drain down!*" Morland yelled from across the room. Workers scurried to move equipment and supplies to higher ground and to fix the gutter, but no one addressed the drainage. "*Somebody cut that fuckin' drain down!*" she shouted again, her eyes flashing wide.

Scrambling, I found a handsaw. Little bits of white plastic shot through the air as the metal teeth ripped into the pipe. Crouched on the ground, half of my body lay outside the basement door. Cold rain rushed down my back. Water dripped down soggy strands of hair onto my face. The saw finally sliced through the last of the pipe, which toppled over, allowing the water to recede into a vortex. Crisis was averted, but tension hovered in the air. Everyone resumed work as if nothing had happened, but the stress to get the job done was taking a toll.

For weeks, the ferry shuttled me back and forth for more pointing, laying brick, touching up paint, and light plaster repair. Fall was ending, which meant it was time

Learning about the lime cycle while on the job at 86 Main. PHOTO BY COLIN EVANS.

to resume work on the Loring House. But how to put up a ceiling had eluded me, and there was still the matter of gathering supplies.

I asked Colin if Morland would sell me some of her lime putty, which no hardware store in the country carried. Running low, they didn't want to part with any. "Call Fabio," Colin said, giving me the number for a traditional mason on the mainland.

On the last ferry home, I sat on the open deck at the back of the boat. Under a clear sky, an easterly wind blew salt spray on my face. My hair whipped in all directions as the sun warmed me. The island shrank in the distance until nothing remained but the sea.

Back at the house, I decided to make my own lime putty. At a local beach, shells that had washed ashore filled an old canvas duffel bag. Round, with flat white bases and small openings like tiny slippers, they had come from sea snails. Sand and stringy, dark seaweed clung to the bottom of the bag, as sea water leeched through the fabric. The stale, sulphury smell of low tide permeated the air.

Into the firepit on the Loring House patio went a beehive stack of logs and, in the center, the mollusk shells. After the pile burned down, black ashes yielded a white powder and pieces of charred shell, which I transferred to a glass baking dish, then added water. At first nothing happened. Then slowly the white paste bubbled, a twisting ribbon of steam rising from it. It worked! When cool, the slaked lime filled a quarter of a small Mason jar. At that rate, it would take months to make enough lime for the bathroom ceiling.

Better to call Fabio. He lived on the North Shore, but we had met briefly on Nantucket. I told him I wanted to buy some of his lime putty.

"What you going to use it for?" he asked in a heavy Italian accent, sounding defensive. The question surprised me, as did the strange feeling that I needed to justify the purchase. But explaining the project in detail put him at ease.

"I have what you need. Come by the house and pick it up."

In Salem, an hour north around Massachusetts Bay, his yellow colonial house lay at the end of a long driveway, behind a row of tall hedges, atop a hill. When I arrived, he was smoking a cigarette in the yard. Inside the house, he showed me some of his work, including an arched doorway made of terracotta brick and plaster. Then he steered me down a long staircase to the basement, which contained rows of white buckets stacked to the ceiling, full of imported Italian lime. It had aged for varying time frames, like fine wine or whiskey, some of it ten years old. The greater the age, the more it cost.

"It's closer to pure calcium carbonate than anything you going to find on the market here," he said, as if we were talking about hard drugs. "It's low fired. That's how they used to make it, not like what you get when you buy lime made in the States. It has a microcrystalline structure that breaks down. The quality gets better with time, more workable, you know."

I nodded, with no idea what he was talking about. I politely requested two buckets, which he set by the door. "One more thing," I said, "I need hair."

Because lime on its own proves brittle, colonial craftsmen added animal hair to their plaster. The long slender fibers strengthened it and reduced shrinkage, which minimized cracking as it dried. Fabio's eyes glimmered as he directed me to another corner of the basement, this one piled with stacks of boxes, each filled with tiny bushels of hair bound with pieces of string. "What kind of hair you want?"

Unsure how to answer, I picked up one of the bushels and brushed it against my palm. It felt oddly familiar.

On one of my childhood hikes in the Green Mountains of Vermont, our small band of friends had come across a maggot-ridden deer carcass. Curious, we poked it with a stick, holding our noses to mask the nauseating stench of ammonia. A tuft of fur lay on the ground nearby. I brushed it against my palm. To that point, new adventures had filled our days, with little time left to consider our own mortality. But seeing the deer taught us that the forest could be a cruel and indiscriminate place. The ecosystem had balance, and our existence was fragile. There was an impermanence for all things.

"That's goat hair," Fabio said, breaking the moment's silence, pointing to the bushel in my hand, his eyes still glimmering.

Studying goat hair in the depths of a stranger's cellar—my pursuit of becoming a preservationist had taken my life for an odd turn. Looking up at this purveyor of old-world plastering supplies, there was only one thing left to say.

"I'll take two bushels."

FIRST, the moldy drywall in the bathroom had to come down. My utility knife cut a small square in one corner, wide enough to fit the end of my crowbar, which slid underneath it. The board separated, breaking into pieces that clattered to the floor. Countless spores floated through the air, hazing the room and making me sneeze uncontrollably. Beneath the drywall, contractors had kept the original strips of wooden lath, which needed only shoring up.

I gathered a bag of sand, a bucket of lime, and the bushels of hair. Into a plastic mixing tub went a cup of sand, the rich textured grains sliding across the smooth surface of the basin. Eroding through time, this sand had washed ashore on the New England coastline, fighting the tide that tried to pull it back out to sea. Tiny shell fragments, fossils of marine life, had settled on the ocean floor, gradually forming the lime that joined the sand in the tub. In went the goat hair, all of it mixing together with a wood-handled hoe pushed back and forth, the rhythm like lapping waves. It all connected somehow. The joys of the ritual, perfect for a preservationist, reminded me not of the universe's impermanence but, instead, the reason to resist it.

The end of a rectangular trowel scooped up some of the plaster, tendrils of hair sprouting in all directions, and set it on a thin square tool called a hawk that my other hand held like a painter's palette. The material smelled chalky. The trowel worked the plaster into a ball and lifted it over my head. Every muscle in my arm pushed up, then out, smearing it across the wooden strips above. The pressure squeezed water from the lime, giving the material the firmness of cream cheese. Over and over, the trowel wedged mushy plaster deeper into the gaps between the lath, forcing it into the cavity beneath the second story floorboards, where it curled over. As the curls, called keys, hardened, they locked the ceiling in place.

I worked my way across the room, the occasional section peeling away, splattering on the floor and dotting the walls with dribbling white beads. By the time I reached the other end, the first passes were growing lighter, drying. The trowel left small track marks in the surface, which I could smooth later, after it set. The new plaster warmed the room.

My aching arm hung from a sore shoulder that I rotated a few times to loosen. *OK, the hard part's over*, I reassured myself.

For Thomas Loring III, plastered ceilings represented refinement, upward mobility, a transition away from the homes of earlier colonists, which had exposed-frame ceilings. For me, it also meant mobility and transition but in a different way. Several months ago, I landed on Nantucket with no plastering experience and, in my new profession, no status. But in the tradition of Richard Macy, master builder, I had worked with lime and, like him, was becoming

Plastering the bathroom ceiling was shoulder-killing work. PHOTO BY LIZ BAILEY.

self-reliant. The plaster hung overhead in high style. It had visibly improved the Loring House, a piece of its original texture restored. The caustic lime that had burned my eye would keep the mold from returning.

Two more months had passed, leaving thirteen to ready the rest of the house before guests arrived. In the nights that followed, my head hummed with worry that the ceiling would fall before setting completely, a risk when using traditional plastering techniques. Each morning, I braced myself for the worst, but it held.

Then one night, an alarming crash woke Liz and me from a dead sleep. Leaping from bed, I rushed to the bathroom, expecting to find crumbled plaster all over the floor. To my surprise, the ceiling remained intact. But relief quickly turned to panic. What had caused the sound? Had someone broken into the house? Heart racing, I grabbed the black metal flashlight from the closet, its weight heavy in my hand. It could fend off an intruder if it came to that. Tiptoeing into the hallway, then to the stairs, I clenched the stair rail and crept softly down the steps, stopping on the landing to listen for any noises.

Silence.

Scanning the room, my eye caught a shadow. *Was that a person?* The darkness made it hard to tell. Motionless, my eyes adjusted, and the shape came into view. The dinnerware that we planned to use at our Thanksgiving feast lay scattered on the floor, shattered into a thousand pieces.

IV.

The
Black Art

As iron is eaten away by rust, so the envious
are consumed by their own passion.

—Antisthenes

"I HAVE A SURPRISE FOR YOU," LIZ SAID, SITTING
on the stairs as I walked through the door.

Before I could respond, a cat poked from around
the corner and eyed me, startled. The lanky Siamese had
pointy dark ears, sharp blue eyes, and a long whiskered
face. It looked as if the five-year-old beige female hadn't
eaten in weeks.

"Guess what I got?" Liz asked, smiling.

Our existing Siamese, an old man named Mango, spent
entire days on floor vents that blew hot air on him. Mice
were overrunning the house. For months, Liz had been
talking about getting a younger cat to deal with the issue.
She picked this one while I was on Nantucket so I couldn't
protest. The new cat hid under a wooden bench in the entryway. As I went to pet her, she shot into the living room and
started climbing inside the chimney. Shouting, Liz chased

her, plucking her from the brick before she went too far. We took her upstairs and closed her in the bedroom. If she went back up the flue, we might not be able to get her out. I liked the cat, but she was going to be trouble. We named her Ruthie.

Above the fireplace that Ruthie tried to scale sat a built-in cabinet with two shelves and panel doors. The original hinges had come off long ago, but the replacement hinges didn't work. The doors stuck open. Liz had decorated the shelves with some of our best wedding gift dinnerware: two rows of plates as the backdrop and crystal Champagne flutes as the centerpiece. In the middle of the night, Ruthie, exploring her new home, had launched herself from the floor to the shelf and cleared the entire display like a bowling ball landing a strike. Crashing to the brick hearth, the crystal shattered into razor-sharp fragments. A feeling of ambivalence came over me as I stood in the darkness in my underwear. There was no intruder to fend off, which was a relief, but our wedding gifts had been ruined. I shone the light at the cupboard.

"I've got to fix those doors."

A BLACKSMITH had forged the original hinges from iron, fastening them with wrought nails. The spirit of those hinges, though long gone, remained. Paint layers had built up around the edges where they once hung, like the chalk outline at a crime scene. Several rooms of the Loring House still had original H hinges, which resemble the shape of the letter, and plenty of good antique shops sold them. The thought of buying a set crossed my mind, but the words of Richard Macy's grandson nagged at me: "The ironwork, the nails excepted, he generally wrought with his own hands." I should try to make them myself.

On Nantucket, contractors in 86 Main had installed a hand-forged stair rail—the ends hammered thin and curled into scrollwork, the balusters twisted into spirals—all of it the work of a skilled craftsman. "Who made these?" I had asked.

"Tony Millham," said one of the workers.

A blacksmith, Millham specialized in reproducing early American hardware, so he seemed like a good person to call.

"Hello?" said a gruff voice.

"Is this Tony?" I asked.

"Yes, it is," he said.

I explained who I was and what I wanted to do. "Would you be open to showing me how to make a set?"

"H hinges?" he said, considering the possibility. "I don't have an order for any, but I suppose I can make 'em. Just call me a few days before you want to come by."

Millham lived in Westport, a quiet seaside town on the southern tip of the Massachusetts coastline. A string of winding country roads crawled through windswept hills, over which stretches of stone walls tumbled. Old farmhouses lay scattered across the landscape, their shingles battered by salt air. Trees surrounded Millham's secluded house and workshop, set back from the road. A small sign featuring a hand-painted anvil hung next to the door. After I pulled into the driveway, rummaging for a notepad, a thin figure flashed across the rearview mirror, then disappeared.

Around Millham's workshop stood large pieces of industrial equipment painted in a muted gray and blotted in patches of machine oil. Lines of hammers and tongs flanked metal cabinets containing rows of labeled drawers. On the shop floor, a coating of black dust lurked under table legs and in corners, just beyond reach of the broom. At the center of the room, the slender brick stack of the forge descended from the ceiling, its base jutting out like a giant foot that had stepped through the roof. Under a vent hood, a shallow pan held a pile of black, pitted, craggy coal, each piece the size of a pebble. In the background, a radio murmured classical music, and on the wall hung a large poster of a flasher opening his trench coat to a sculpture in a park. "Expose yourself to art," the caption read.

"So you want to make some H hinges?" Millham said. In his seventies and lean, he had a gray mustache and a slight arch in his back from years of hunching over an anvil. He rooted around in a bin in a corner of the shop and shuffled back, holding a handful of thin metal sheets. "This is A36, a mild steel."

With shears, he trimmed one of the sheets into a halved H, clamped it in a vise, and hammered the protruding end into a barrel. Bringing that piece and several more to the forge, he flicked a wall switch. An electric fan forced air into the center of the coal pan, the rush of oxygen keeping the fire hot. He lit the end of a welding torch into a blue-pointed flame and placed it over the forge. When a low continuous fire burned at the center of the coal, he buried the pieces of steel under it, and we waited.

"This isn't how they used to do it, but it's a lot faster," he said, a sly grin drawing out across his face.

Millham's father had worked as a lawyer, a profession his brother followed, but the casework didn't appeal to Tony. He wanted to make things. In his twenties, he met an eclectic group of craftsmen who restored old houses and had what he called "old house soul." They offered him a job making reproduction hardware, fitting historic buildings with hinges, latches, and gates. But in middle age, he lost interest in it, going back to school to become a geologist. "Geology is like blacksmithing," he said. "It's heat, pressure, and minerals—all the same thing, really." He took a job designing a septic system testing facility on Cape Cod, but the desire to make things kept tugging at him. "I cut my schedule to four days to blacksmith again on Fridays and Saturdays." Soon he was back at it full time.

With tongs, he pulled the steel from the fire, the metal glowing white-hot, set it on the anvil, and beat it with a large hammer. Sparks flew in all directions. The liquified steel of the overlapping section of the barrel melded together with the body of the hinge into a solid piece, producing a hinge stronger than mass-produced, store-bought reproductions made today. With indifference, he tossed it aside, the

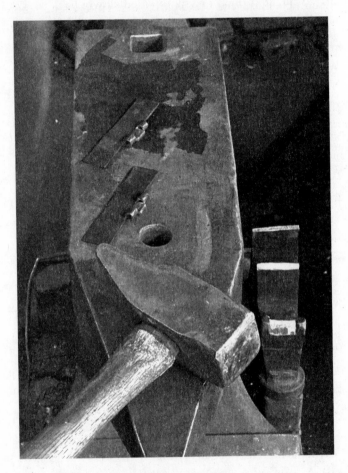

Millham worked the hinges at his shop
until the two halves fit together.

hinge landing on the concrete floor, so it could cool while he started the next one. The glow faded slowly back to a dull gray. When the metal of the second piece had cooled, Millham cut and filed the two pieces until the halves fit together, working each one at different stations around the shop. I followed him, took notes, snapped pictures, and asked questions. He gave long answers, approaching ironwork as a scholar and tradesman. He explained the how-to first, then descended into the science and philosophy of metalwork, as though he were extracting the explanations from a cavern deep in the recesses of his mind. Between answers, he told stories. At one point, he looked away, his eyes distant. "I made a good living," he said, aware that his best years lay behind him.

Hammering a pin in the barrel joined the two halves. He swiveled them back and forth, repeating the process until he had made a complete set. After drilling holes for the nails, his curled, blackened fingers reached toward me, clenching the hinges. "Let's call it fifty bucks."

He took the bills and glanced at the clock on the wall, his way of saying it was time for me to go.

✢ ✢ ✢ ✢

LOCAL ANTIQUE shops occasionally turned up a set of tongs; an old, saddled anvil; or other blacksmithing tools. They proved scarce, though, so I bought whatever I could find. But I still needed a forge.

Millham had modeled his, made of brick, after an

eighteenth-century design, adding an electric blower. To heat iron, Richard Macy would've used a hand-powered bellows to keep his fire hot. Made from two teardrop-shaped planks of wood—hinged at the front, connected by a leather strip on the side—it expanded and contracted air through a narrow tube, like a lung. Short on time, I couldn't build anything so elaborate. The Industrial Age had yielded smaller, portable forges cast from iron, the bellows giving way to hand-crank blowers. These portable forges still turned up at flea markets and antique stores, so I set out to find one.

On an early fall Saturday, Liz and I drove up to Vermont to see the leaves changing color. In the crisp autumn air, the earthy scent of fallen leaves mingled with the smoky aromas of chimney fire. The mountains were erupting in organic fireworks of red, orange, and yellow. Soon the trees would shed their variegated coats and huddle together, shivering in the cold winds of winter. We stopped in Quechee, known for its 165-foot gorge carved by a glacier some 13,000 years ago. Streams of visitors parked in a lot, then walked onto a bridge suspended over the chasm. We joined them for a moment, peering over the rail into the long drop below.

Heading into a rustic building, crowds of tourists eyed an array of Vermont-made products. After sipping pumpkin spice coffees, sampling cheeses, and eating maple sugar candy, we wandered to an antique mall next door. It contained row after row of booths, each a glimpse into the mind of its proprietor, their obsessions literally on display. Some collections revealed a uniform pattern. One booth offered only antique furniture, another old toys; one military collectibles, another only kitchenware; and so on. Others displayed random piles for buyers to scavenge. For years, many of the items had lain in attics or basements, buried under layers of dust before they were dredged up. Whiffs of mothballs and musty air wafted around us, interrupting the pleasant smell of old barn wood. We trod each aisle, slowly scanning the aged merchandise.

Under a table, an object on the floor caught my eye. It lay buried under a heap of stuff, which I knelt to clear. Wrestling it free, I discovered a small blacksmith's forge. Cast from iron and shaped like a large bowl, it sat on three slender, curved legs. Mounted underneath, a round casing that resembled a handheld blow-dryer housed a fan blade that channeled air through a tube to a grate in the bottom of the pan. A jagged gear with a wooden handle turned a leather belt that powered the strange-looking contraption. Cranking it ground the small, heavy forge to life, a light stream of air blowing on my hand. A small white tag attached with a piece of string listed the price, which was within my budget. Sold.

Next on the list: coal and iron.

TODAY, AMERICA imports most of its iron. Ore, the natural rock containing the metal, lies buried deep in the earth's crust. Miners must extract it with heavy equipment. When the Loring House was built, blacksmiths used bog ore, found on the surface. Bog ore forms in a chemical reaction caused when decayed vegetation mixes with iron salts in stream beds. "When there is a strata of greensands or marls which carry a soluble iron under the soil, water seeps through the marls, causing the iron in the solution to rise to the surface of the water where it oxidizes. The oxide is deposited along the banks of the stream. The deposits mix with mud and turn into thick, red, and rocky masses of ore," according to iron historians Herbert, Peter, and Nancy Schiffer.

In North America, colonists considered iron from the start. In 1585, the Raleigh expedition discovered iron ore on Roanoke Island in what became North Carolina. By 1608, colonists were exporting bog ore from Jamestown, Virginia, to England. Thomas Morton wrote of the existence of "iron stone" in New England in 1632, and in 1646, the Company of Undertakers for the Iron Workes in New England, led by John Winthrop the Younger—Puritan, magistrate, and son of the founding governor of the Massachusetts Bay Colony—funded the first ironworks in the country, which they named Hammersmith.

From the outset, Hammersmith experienced trouble. "In encouraging the setting up of ironworks, the Puritan magistrates were opening a Pandora's box, whose contents would undercut many of the things for which they stood," wrote ironworks historian Edward Hartley. They built the plant on a grander scale than the burgeoning economy could support, and the rough-and-tumble iron workers frequently clashed with strict Puritan values. "Instead of drawing out bars of iron for the country's use, there was hammered out nothing but contention and lawsuits," observed William Hubbard, a colonial clergyman and historian. According to court records, John Turner, one such worker, was "overtaken by drink," threatened to kill a man, and stabbed his daughter-in-law. Henry Stiche broke the head of Richard Bayly, according to testimony, and Richard Pray received a fine for cursing, beating his wife, and contempt of court. Despite these setbacks, an early description of the dirty, noisy plant called it "as good as any worke England doth afoarde." After a few decades, though, debts outweighed profits. With heavy costs, modest production, and disappointing sales, its doors closed.

Covering the abandoned equipment, falling leaves decomposed into a thick layer of soil that buried the ironworks, which history forgot. In 1948, archaeologist Roland Robbins, known for discovering the site of Henry Thoreau's cabin at Walden Pond, went looking for it. The intact ironworks lay undisturbed underground. Archaeologists uncovered it, and a complete recreation went up nearby. Called the Saugus Iron Works National Historic Site, it serves as a museum operated by the National Park Service. On a sundrenched autumn day, Liz and I went to see whether anyone there knew where I could find wrought iron.

Isolated from rows of residential housing, the museum and its waterwheel-powered mills sit in a sprawl of open space in the heart of suburbia. While we waited for the tour guide, another couple and their young son joined us. Dressed in a crisp olive-green uniform and wide-brimmed hat, the park ranger arrived exactly on the hour. After a brief overview of ironwork in America, he signaled toward a narrow path: "Follow me."

We dutifully filed in line behind him. Down the path, a stone trapezoidal structure, taller than a house, appeared in the distance. On one side, it had a sloped wooden roof, and at its peak a long narrow timber bridge connected it to a hilltop. It looked like a giant detached chimney.

"This is the blast furnace," said the guide. Silently we gathered at the foot of the structure. The ranger pointed to the hill and the bridge that ran to the top of the furnace. "Workers brought three raw materials over the charging bridge and loaded them into the chimney of the furnace: iron ore, charcoal, and gabbro, a type of local stone."

The young boy in the group was fidgeting already.

"The charcoal was made from wood by workers known as colliers. They piled the wood in mounds and covered it with dirt and leaves, setting it on fire in a low charring flame, standing guard day and night. The ore was picked from the bogs and the stone quarried near what today is Nahant."

Now the boy was tugging on his mother's pantleg.

"Once the charcoal was lit, a 3,000-degree fire was kept burning for twenty-four hours, melting the iron and the gabbro. The stone was used as a flux, separating the impurities in the ore, which would float to the surface while the dense iron sank to the bottom, like oil and water." The guide indicated a small opening at the bottom of the furnace, motioning for us to move closer, then pointed at the sand-covered ground. A long, dug-out channel ran from the door, with several rows of offshoots. "The furnace was tapped, the waste drawn to the side, which hardened into slag. The good iron flowed into these channels. Because they resemble baby piglets feeding from their mother, the bars were called 'pig iron.' "

My mind drifted, imagining one of the early ironworkers grunting his way up the hill, his wheelbarrow weighted with rocks. Reaching the top of the chimney, a gaping inferno belching smoke and soot, he tottered to the edge. Ensuring that he had good footing to keep from tumbling into the fiery pit, he tipped his load into the unbearable heat. From the base of the furnace, with the tap opened, iron flowed like lava, a viscous stream of molten metal slithering down the narrow sand channels where it cooled.

The ranger corralled us under the wood roof jutting from the side of the furnace, snapping me back to the present. He pointed at a giant hammer, its handle the size of a telephone pole, its head the size of a small refrigerator. "This is called a trip hammer. It draws out the bars of iron." He signaled to another park ranger on the nearby hill. "We're going to demonstrate how it works. A warning, it's going to be loud."

The second ranger opened a small gate, directing water from a stream into a wooden chute that poured over a large wheel. The hammer came alive, jumping up and down, each strike landing a clap so thunderous that we had to cover our ears. After several minutes, the second ranger cut the water supply, halting the process. My ears rang.

"Does anyone have any questions?"

My hand went up. "Do you know where to find wrought iron today?"

The ironworks reproduction was fully functional, but they didn't make or sell iron. The ranger had heard of a business that did, though.

Lyons Iron, named for Rob Lyon, its proprietor, stood next to a miniature horse farm in Brookfield, Massachusetts. A short, energetic man with milky white hair and a trimmed beard, Lyon ran the business from his house. He had worked as a blacksmith at an area living-history museum, acquiring and reselling hand-forged antiques as a side business. Finding buyers for his collection had become a new, full-time business. In an old barn behind his house, his store teemed with old fireplace tools, door latches, pots, and kettles, everything orderly. On a wall-mounted pegboard hung dozens of hinges. If the blacksmithing didn't go as planned, having some of these as extras seemed like a good backup plan. Lyon hovered, quick to give a lengthy backstory on each piece that I examined as I worked my way around the room.

He did most of the talking, and I listened, barely able to wedge a word in. Then he paused. "What are you looking for?"

I put down the pitted black cooking pot in my hands. "I want to make a hinge from scratch, and I need wrought iron."

A fire kindled in his eyes. "Come with me."

He took me through a side door, through the dining room, down a flight of stairs, and into the basement. The main room overflowed with old ironwork, everything organized by category and stacked in rows. Compartments abutted it, some no more than shallow crawl spaces, each filled with metal relics. It was like entering a pharaoh's tomb. One corner had stacks of unused iron, square bars, round bars, and sheet metal, all in various lengths.

"These almost got thrown in a dumpster," he said, pointing to one of the piles.

I rummaged through it, selecting several thin sheets of metal.

BACK AT the house, the sun was shining, and the frost on the grass was melting into tiny droplets that gleamed in the light. A breeze rustled through the trees, and a burst of leaves descended around me in all directions. My warm breath condensed in the cool air. A hand truck helped me wheel an anvil, the forge, a box of coal purchased from a specialty shop, and a handful of tools to the same corner of the yard where I'd hewn the beam for the timber frame repair. After trimming the iron into a halved H and hammering the barrel over in a vice, just as Millham had done, it was time to light the coal.

While assembling the materials, I thought back to a camping trip at The Rock, where I first learned how to build a fire. Our small band gathered stones, bark, twigs, and logs. After setting the stones in a ring, we dug out the center of our firepit with a stick, sending hordes of insects scattering across the moist soil. In the center, we piled white, ribbony coils of birch bark marked with rows of black dashes that looked like the paper on which we practiced cursive at school. I thumbed the wheel of a pocket lighter, metal grinding against flint to spark a flame. The wispy ends of the bark crinkled, and the pile went up in a blaze. Thick gray smoke drifted upward, folding over as it rose. We hastily added the wood, starting with twigs and graduating to logs, occasionally blowing on the embers until the fire burned bright. That fire smelled different than the barbeque grills of backyard cookouts in my youth. It had no tinge of lighter fluid, no petroleum-based kerosene, just a pleasant, pure, rich, smoky fragrance.

For the forge, lighting the bituminous coal, the type preferred by blacksmiths, had distinctions of its own. Strips of brown grocery bags served as starters. The coal took longer to catch than wood, emitting a sulfurous, rotten egg smell. After the small mound of coal caught, I nestled the iron into the center and waited, checking it periodically with a set of tongs. Its color turned gray, red, then bright orange.

Cranking the blower handle made a faint whirring sound, and the coals burned bright. The metal turned buttery yellow. Sparks shot from the center of the forge, indicating that the iron had begun to liquefy. I used tongs to pull it from the fire and hold it firmly on the anvil. The first hammer blow landed right in the middle, clean. The metal crumpled, and glowing bits of slag arced through the air. Several hit my bare arm and felt like tiny pin jabs. As I hammered, trying to roll the metal into a cylinder, the tool skipped around. The metal was cooling with each passing second, and haste made me hit the barrel by mistake. The rounded metal collapsed, flattened, ruined.

My second attempt developed a rhythm: three beats against the heated iron, then a fourth against the anvil, the hammer bouncing and ringing. *Tink, tink, tink, tiiing. Tink, tink, tink, tiiing.* The strange music worked. The overlapping ends of the barrel, or knuckles, melded together properly into a solid piece. One piece cooled on a flat stone while I made the next until a complete set lay before me. When they all had cooled, I cut and filed them, working each until the halves fit, then hammered in pins and drilled holes for nails.

Removing the doors of the built-in cabinet above the fireplace was going to prove tricky, though. Unable to close, the doors jutted out, making it hard to reach the existing hinges with a screwdriver. Paint completely caked the existing screws, which had replaced the original wrought nails. With both hands, the slotted screwdriver twisted hard, and the screw spun out. As the hinge loosened, tiny chips of paint broke away, exposing half a dozen different layers of color. Hinges removed, it was time to close the doors, probably for the first time in at least a century. But in more than 300 years, the house frame had shifted so far from square that the doors didn't fit anymore. The ends needed planing down to line up again.

The new hardware matched the paint outline of the originals, settling into the recesses like pieces of a jigsaw puzzle. A handful of rosehead nails—so-named because the peen marks on each head resemble flower petals—tacked the hinges onto each cupboard door and fastened the doors to the frame. After a little planing, the doors opened and closed exactly as they once did. Success.

For the builders of the Loring House, turning local bog-picked rocks into iron must have seemed like alchemy. The metal dramatically changed the course of human history from the start of the Iron Age, and it continued to do so for the colonists who had come to America. More than stone or bronze, the material's properties struck a balance between strength and pliability, making it essential for survival. For me, iron also found a useful purpose at home. The cupboard doors now closed, keeping our valuables safe—if not from burglars, then at least from a curious cat.

OUR GUESTS were coming in a little more than ten months. The pall of winter brought a chill to the house. It rained less, and the air grew dry. The wood in the house shrank, and the floorboard nails reared their heads en masse again. My lips chapped, my skin dried and itched, and my sinuses became irritated. The air of one bitterly cold December morning stung my nose as my breath condensed before my eyes. My mouth tasted like paste.

Rolling from bed, I pulled a sweater over my head, shuffled into slippers, and staggered downstairs to the kitchen for some water. Glass under spigot, I turned the faucet handle. Nothing. I swung the handle back and forth, concern quickly waking me. My hand pushed the handle to the open position and kept it there. Still no water.

Outside the kitchen window, a thick layer of frost had crystalized on all the plants. A sheen of white sparkled in the sun. The night before, the temperature had dropped well below freezing. Standing in the biting cold, empty glass in hand, it finally dawned on me.

Oh no, the pipes.

V.

The Stone Whisperer

Nothing is built on stone; all is built on sand,
but we must build as if the sand were stone.

—*Jorge Luis Borges*

O NE BLUSTERY GRAY WINTER DAY, BRYSON and I went for a walk behind the house. The nylon fabric of my puffy down jacket rubbed at the sleeves, buzzing faintly. We followed a path through the grass the horses had trampled when running to the open field, churning it to mud. Frozen into a lumpy, ankle-twisting crust, the hardened dirt crunched under our feet. We stepped cautiously.

The wind swirled, gusts swatting at us, until we reached the blue gate and ducked into the respite of trees. We followed the trail, accompanied by a stone wall running in the same direction. The wall was crude, its face rough. Jagged, haphazardly laid stones poked in all directions, with large gaps among them, some so wide that my hand fit through to the other side. In some places, rocks had fallen out and sat alone, tumbled from their intended hollows. Green lichens blotted the long stretch of gray wall as if dabbed on by the brush of a landscape painter.

The wall continued into the forest, leading the way, until we reached a clearing in which a large tree had fallen the season before. My chainsaw had cut it to pieces, revealing eighty rings or so and the buttermilk color of the wood, which had faded after a year of exposure to air. One of the largest in the forest, the tree and its rings indicated that the land had begun rewilding less than a century ago. This rich diversity of plant and animal life didn't occur in open fields where livestock graze. In the last hundred years or so, the land had reverted closer to how it looked before Europeans arrived. The stone wall ran farther into the forest, deep into the thick brush, beyond sight, but we turned back toward the house.

On the walk home, the wall and the countless hours it took to construct it occupied my mind. Before the Industrial Age, that kind of effort seemed impossible. How had the wall come to be?

As I stood in the kitchen, with no water pouring from the faucet, panic welled up inside me. Mango, my old Siamese, was lying on an air vent on the floor. He looked up with a blank expression: *Sorry, can't help you.* The situation felt alarming, but nothing indicated that the pipes had burst— yet. I turned up the thermostat and rushed to the store to buy a space heater to put under the sink, hoping it would buy me time.

Back home, I tore open the box, sliding the heater from its protective cardboard. Bits of loose packing foam drifted to the floor. Ignoring the lengthy instruction manual, I plugged in the heater, cranked the dial to the highest setting, and shoved it under the sink. It came to life with a whir, and a stream of hot air flowed from its metal louvers.

I made my way to the cellar to follow the water lines. In a crawl space under the kitchen floor, the black metal flashlight revealed no obvious signs of a problem. At the other end of the basement, the main water line came in from the street, branching in every conceivable direction. Suspended by hooks nailed to floor joists, two copper pipes hung over head, disappearing into darkness. There was no getting around it: I had to go into the hole.

The narrow opening stood at shoulder level. A kitchen chair gave me the necessary leg-up to climb into it, shimmying on my stomach, slithering in the dirt, no room to turn back. Pulled close to my chest, my arms wriggled me forward. Above me, sharp, rusty nails protruded from the floorboards, while dozens of spindly brown spiders crawled overhead, inches from my face. It felt like being buried alive.

At the end of the trench, the space opened into a hollow, which freed my arms and legs. Tiny rays of light pierced the blackness, and wind whipped my cheeks. To install the drain line for the sink, workers had ripped a hole in the foundation, but they didn't repair it properly. The deck, built off the back of the kitchen, hid it from view. With no barrier to block it, the frigid winter air assaulted the pipes

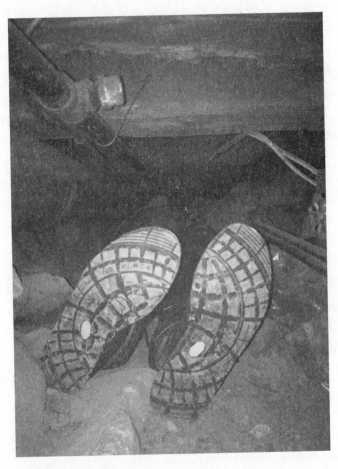

Shimmying into the crawl space felt like being buried alive. PHOTO BY LIZ BAILEY.

from all sides, all season long. This section of foundation consisted of a single, thin course of stone. Deep in the bowels of the house, which had swallowed me whole, I lay prone for several minutes, processing the situation. The foundation needed rebuilding.

A search online led me to a class that offered instruction in the art of dry-laid stonework, the same technique that Richard Macy and the builders of the Loring House had used. But the class took place outside, so the earliest available date fell in springtime. Fearful of rumors about space heaters burning down houses, I snaked a heating cable into the hole, coiled it around the pipes, and plugged it in. That bought me time for warmer weather to arrive.

The cold of winter and dwindling hours of daylight slowed the rhythms of work. The thought of idleness unsettled me, so a trip to the local library supplied a stack of books on geology and stonework and a chance to do some homework before professional instruction began.

ACCORDING TO geologists, earth stone originated 4.6 billion years ago. In its first 500 million years, called the Hadean Eon, our planet accumulated from fragments—comets, debris, dust—of other exploded planets. Asteroids and radioactive decay generated tremendous heat that melted the newly forming sphere. Earth's interior liquefied and volatile gases, including carbon dioxide and nitrogen, boiled to the surface.

"To the Puritans, hell was a place of eternal damnation, hot, dark, and sulfurous. However, in geologic terms, hell is not a place but a time," wrote geologist Robert Thorson. Lava oozed to the surface, cooling into basalt, a type of igneous rock, while heavier compounds seeped downward, forming the planet's core. Vapors turned to mist, which condensed into rain that created today's oceans, lakes, and streams. Into those bodies of water settled mineral fragments and fossilized debris, which accreted into layers of sedimentary stone, including sandstone and limestone. Continents formed and collided with one another, pushing surface rock to the center of the planet, where extreme pressure and heat reshaped it into varieties of metamorphic stone. Ice ages came, and giant glaciers ploughed the planet's crust, churning rocks from each of those three categories. In New England, Richard Macy and the builders of the Loring House found and worked with basalt, gneiss, granite, schist, and slate.

THE HOUSE'S pipes survived the winter, and time came for the stonework class in West Rutland, Vermont, not far from the woods of my childhood. As with many small towns across America, industry had dried up, replaced by an artist community. An old industrial building that lay down a long, quiet, gravel road had become the home of a carving and sculpture studio where the class took place. A small set of steps led to two doors that stood propped open. The building, an old brick loading dock, had a large, open floor plan. White painted beams ran overhead, anchored with thick metal brackets, each pierced with giant iron bolts.

A middle-aged woman wearing glasses welcomed me and directed me to a sign-in sheet. "The restrooms are in the back," she said, pointing to the opposite end of the room. "There's also coffee if you'd like some."

Steaming cup in hand, I sat at a long table amid an eclectic bunch. To my left, a man in striped overalls and a bandana stood against the wall, looming silently. Across from me sat an older man with a beard but no mustache, in the style of an Amish elder, accompanied by a stout woman with short hair and colorful dangling earrings who talked incessantly. To my right, sat a short bald man who had grown his mustache long and curled its ends. "I'm Barry," he said, shaking my hand.

After several minutes, the woman who had welcomed me joined the group along with a tall man who held a stack of papers under his arm. They sat at the center of the table. "Let's go around the table and say who you are and where you're from," she said in a jittery voice.

Reluctantly we followed her instruction. At the end of the round robin, our focus shifted to the tall man. "I'm your instructor," he said, in a slow, deep voice, "My name is Dan Snow."

Snow grew up in Brattleboro, Vermont. His mother worked as a nurse and his father as an advertising manager at the local newspaper. When young, Snow juggled interests in sculpture, photography, painting, drawing, and alpine skiing, describing himself as an "athlete artist." After moving to Brooklyn to attend Pratt Institute's Industrial Design Program, he dropped out to assist a sculptor in Manhattan. "The school part seemed pale compared to the sculpture stuff," he said. Homesick, he returned to Vermont, taking a job as a general contractor restoring old houses. Over time, he cut back what he didn't like until only stonework remained.

"Construction is like art," said Snow. "It's all about making space. Loose stone offers freedom, exploration. How can I make something complex from something simple?" Snow laid stone without mortar, carefully considering the placement of each piece. "In time, my work will be overrun by growth. The forest eats things up. Root systems dislodge things. Things last only as long as somebody cares about them."

Snow built walls and repaired old foundations, but his true passion lay in using stone to create art installations. "He knew he wanted to be an artist from an early age," said his wife, Elin. "He takes his inspiration from nature, being in it, thinking about it, studying it." Mundane jobs afforded him the opportunity to tackle more expressive projects. A journalist had dubbed him "the stone whisperer." He had short gray hair, carved facial features, and a thin, muscular frame—the agile skier still present. He was wearing a blue button-down shirt and a wide-brimmed straw hat that made him look like a field hand from an Impressionist painting come to life.

Snow passed around several sheets of paper, each depicting a wall from different angles. He held up one of the illustrations, his copy laminated in shiny plastic. "You want to stagger the courses of stone, the same as building a brick wall, and avoid running joints. Staggering the stones will strengthen it." He picked up another drawing from the table. "Set the stones with the weight sloping to the center. This way, gravity will keep them together. Then you want to fill any gaps with smaller stones called hearting. When possible, it's important to set long stones length in. The tendency is to want to lay them with the length running in the direction of the wall, but the wall will be stronger if you lay them across the courses. It ties everything together."

After the presentation, he herded us to the yard, where a truckload of random fieldstone lay behind the building. First, we had to separate it by size, everyone sorting the rocks into piles while Snow dug a long shallow trench and filled it with a thin layer of gravel. "This will help with drainage and prevent frost heaving." At each end of the gravel-filled trench, he staked two wooden frames, each shaped like a blocky A, into the ground and tied a yellow string from end to end, outlining the shape of wall that we were going to build. A slight taper at the top made it harder for frost heaves to topple it, we learned.

We each took up a space along the wall, laying the largest stones first, trying to keep them neatly inside the guidelines. As we worked, Snow hovered, sometimes giving instruction, sometimes working with us. He spoke about building with intuition and listening to the stone. His connection to the material seemed spiritual. We listened intently, like disciples, the field of rock our sanctuary. "I work with stone because stone is so much work. The more engaged I am in working, the freer my thoughts become," he had written in *The Solitary Stoneworker*, more philosophy than how-to.

He was right. In that moment came the realization that the combination of work and thought connected me to my own past. That connection, like the wall, drew a long string between two points of time, each memory an individual stone, creating a single lifetime. Tracing it backward allowed me to understand that the events of my childhood served as building blocks that culminated in what my adult life had become.

In the Green Mountains, on the largest group trip to The Rock to date, we followed a brook, walking single file along its bank. Trees shielded us from the summer sun, but humidity saturated the air. Under the weight of ruck sacks full of supplies, we trekked through the scorching heat. Ferocious mosquitoes bit us every chance they could, leaving red welts where they pierced the skin. My pack trapped sweat against my back, drenching my T-shirt. We eyed the stream, looking for a pool deep enough for us to submerge. We found a wide one, but it looked too shallow to swim in.

"Let's dam it up," came a shout from the crowd.

We piled rocks in a line across the brook, some so heavy that moving them required the efforts of two boys at a time. Despite our exertions, water gushed through the gaps, which, like industrious beavers, we tried to fill with branches and leaves. We slowed the brook enough to raise the water level by a foot, then plunged in. A small waterfall rushed above us, the current forced between two rocks. We took turns dunking our heads underneath it, shocked at first by the ice cream headaches it gave us, then relieved. Working with the stone brought us joy. What we were building would last a long time, I told myself. The Rock and the small stones by the stream had existed long before we had and would be there long after we were gone. But the ever-changing forces of nature would reshape them, too, eroding them away. On a long enough timeline, even stone proves impermanent.

Two decades had passed, yet again I found myself in a group piling rocks. The faces looked different, everyone much older, but the feeling of playfulness remained the same. We all found a rhythm. The Amish-looking man and the stout woman, a married couple, worked together. She stood by their section of wall, delegating orders as he scrambled around the yard. "That one," she said, pointing. He picked up a stone and looked at her for approval. "No, the one next to it!" she barked. He dropped the rock, picked up its neighbor, and brought it to her. They worked like this for most of day.

A few feet from where they stood sat a large block-shaped

stone that looked perfect for a gap I was trying to fill, but it proved too heavy to lift.

"Barry, can you help me move this one?" I asked.

"Sure," he said, stumbling over the loose rock toward me.

We encircled the block and tried to wiggle it free. I wrenched hard on one side, spinning it without realizing that Barry had a finger underneath it.

"Owwwww," he howled, pulling away and flicking his hand back and forth.

"I'm so sorry! Are you alright?" I said, feeling terrible for my carelessness.

"I need a minute, but I'll be fine," he replied, clenching his hand. Even the simple act of moving stones required tremendous focus and awareness.

Despite that setback and other occasional cuts and bruises, the wall grew waist-high by lunchtime. Each of us developed the ability to look at an empty space and find a rock to fit it almost perfectly on the first try. The hours melted away, a receding glacier leaving our small stone wall in its wake. In the afternoon, the mood grew festive. Everyone smiled and laughed. We all were reliving our childhoods. When the wall had reached shoulder height, Snow inspected our work.

"This is good," he said softly.

Pride bubbled among the group. We posed for a photo, everyone standing behind the wall, only heads visible, then said our goodbyes. The structure, we learned, would remain on the property, a monument to our experience that would last as long as somebody cared for it. The day gave me new-found confidence to repair the Loring House foundation.

AN EXPANSION in the 1800s had established the house's current kitchen as an L off the main building. A small overhang from that covered the well, which descended twenty feet to the water table. The kitchen foundation, a single course wide, was sinking, and the roofline at the back dipped sharply at one end. In addition to repairing the damaged section around the pipe, my plan called for strengthening the foundation by increasing its thickness with a second course, making it a double-stack wall.

First, I needed more stone, which the original builders had sourced from the property. When Loring acquired the tract of untamed wilderness, he needed to clear it to graze livestock, which helpfully produced materials for building the house. Farmhands and possibly Loring himself burned small saplings and shrubs and chopped down large trees. To maximize efficiency, a process called girdling stripped a ring of bark from the circumference of a trunk, which subjected the tree to fungal attacks that hollowed it until finally it toppled. "Stately trees, sometimes 400 years old, died standing up," geologist and naturalist Robert Thorson noted.

With a harrow—a metal-toothed tool resembling an A lying flat on the ground—workers broke apart the soil. They lashed the harrow to the yoke between two oxen, and whips drove the animals back and forth in the open field. As the

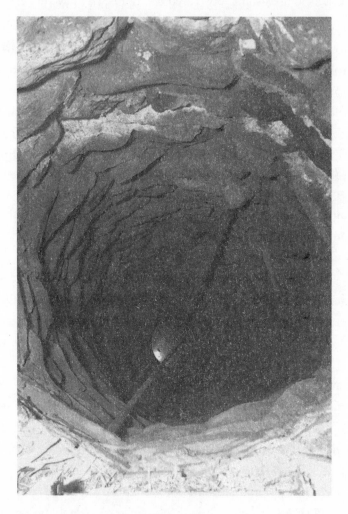

The well.

animals pulled it forward, the harrow's teeth ripped into the spongy loam, dredging up stones in its wake. Fieldhands followed and heaped the rocks into piles. Stones too heavy to lift rolled onto a wooden sled called a stone boat. The oxen went round again, the sled skidding over the trampled earth, until they reached the edge of the field where workers dumped the rocks. They separated out the flattest stones, though, setting them aside for the house's foundation, which importantly kept the rot-prone timber frame off the damp soil. Known as earth-fast structures, New England's earliest houses had no foundations. Their wooden posts went straight into holes dug in the ground. Archeologist David Landon discovered evidence of that method of construction at the Plymouth settlement. The wood, long ago decomposed, left slight discolorations in the soil, dark stains indicating where the posts once stood. But using stone for the foundation, which keeps the wood frame off the ground, prolongs the life of a house.

The account of Richard Macy gathering stone from common land stuck in my mind, making me consider foraging rocks from the property for the repair. The original construction had used up much of the surface stone, but an abundant supply remained. Naturally stony from glacial till, New England soil has a significant component of silt, made of fine sand and clay, prone to frost heaving. When water in the soil freezes, ice expands from its liquid form, creating upward and outward pressure. That pressure slowly nudges rocks to the surface, and the surrounding soil settles when the ground thaws. In time, stones emerge from the soil like zombies rising from graves in a horror movie. Locals call these rocks "New England potatoes."

Heaved stones littered the pasture behind the house. Several hours of poking and prying at them with a shovel generated only a small pile. It was going to take weeks, maybe months, to gather enough. Macy didn't have a holiday deadline, but I did. I needed a new plan.

A few miles from the house, a stone quarry supplied materials for masonry and landscaping projects. Acres of palleted rock stretched in every direction. Inside the building, a large showroom displayed stone patios, firepits, and other modern wonders. Behind a counter, a man in a polo shirt typed furiously at his computer. He looked up at me, expressionless.

"I'm looking for stone to fix the foundation of a really old house," I said.

"We can help you with that," he replied, brandishing an inventory guide from under the counter. He flipped to a page filled with pictures of various types of rock, each labeled with a product name.

Imagining myself walking down to the Loring House cellar, I tried to remember how the foundation stones looked to match them to one of the pictures. "This one looks good," I said after a minute, pointing to a product labeled Yankee Wall Stone.

Several days later, the first day of spring warm enough to wear shorts, the stone appeared in the driveway, a yellow receipt stuck in the side door. A veil of shrink wrap held the perfectly stacked cube of stone together on a pallet. My utility knife sliced open the layers of translucent plastic. Individual rocks went into a blue metal wheelbarrow, each landing with a *smack*, like billiard balls bouncing off one another. The wheelbarrow carried them over the bumps and ruts of the yard, tossing me around, and I spread them on the deck like pieces of a jigsaw puzzle.

Built off the back of the house, the deck obscured the kitchen foundation. My three-foot crowbar pried up several of the deck's boards, creating a long narrow opening. Liz came outside to see how it was going. Another look of concern clouded her face. The deck had become her favorite summer place to sit and relax. Now it had a big hole in the middle of it.

But that hole offered a clear exterior view of the foundation. Sprouting from the dirt, a course of stonework about a foot high ran the length of the eave. It ended where the bottom course of shingles had been nailed to the sheathing. The long chain of interconnected rock ran in a continuous line under the house but bulged in the center, a snake digesting a rodent. Workers had torn open a four-foot section of it for the drain line from the kitchen sink, but they had replaced the stones loosely. Most of that section no longer sat under the frame of the house. The crowbar prodding one of the stones made it jostle with little effort.

A piece of string—stretched from one end of the wall to the other—served as my guideline. A pointed shovel broke easily through the surface soil, cutting into the soft dirt underneath, its texture like packed brown sugar. Piles of earth rose around me as I sunk deeper into an increasingly formidable trench. As I dug, the deeper layers of soil became damp, caking in the treads of my shoes, smearing my hands and knees in rich brown pigment. An earthy smell of decomposing leaves filled the air. A rusty cast-iron pipe poked through the center of the mess, like a giant worm vanishing into the house.

When the entire foundation stood exposed, I removed the top course, through which workers had installed the drain line, setting each stone on the deck behind me. I dismantled one section at a time, working my way to the corner, making sure not to remove so much that the house collapsed. Interlocking courses staggered from ground to sill. The jagged opening, large enough for me to fit through, led to the tunnel into which I had crawled that past winter. Sunlight illuminated the clutter of spiders, moving lethargically beneath the floorboards.

Standing in the trench, I rolled a large flat gneiss rock from the deck. Its streaky blue and white layers melting together, it tumbled into the dirt, skidded down the trench wall—missing my toes by just a few inches—and hit the packed earth with a *thud*. On hands and knees, I slowly pushed it under the frame, each corner ploughing into the ground and building piles of dirt around it. The smooth piece of gneiss, flat on its face and top, had a gradual slope on one side that trailed to the ground. The other side jutted out like the bow of a ship. It needed a complement piece. Examining the stones on the deck, I studied each form, how it curved, where it grew slender or thick, tracing its outline in my mind, until a match revealed itself. I dropped the complement into the trench and pushed the rock under the house until it lined up neatly with the first. Thus began the long process of laying the courses in two parallel rows.

When the stones fit together as closely as they could, it was time to heart them. Small rocks picked from the dirt packed the gaps, which wedged the larger stones firmly against one another. None had room to move. When the two rows had formed properly, I built them higher, setting long rocks across them, length in. I stacked until only small nooks remained between the top course and the sill of the frame, just wide enough to fit my hand, which felt around for crevices and unevenness. But the thought of the house shifting its weight and pinning me beneath it brought to mind the hiker who spent 127 hours in a canyon with his arm trapped under a boulder, forcing him to cut off his own arm with a pocketknife. My hand instinctively pulled away. My hunt for razor-thin stones resumed, and they slid gently under the wood.

With one section complete, I continued to the next, working my way to the corner, careful that the house always had the support it needed. Unlike fitting the new wrought iron hinges into the ghostly outline of their predecessors, this process felt like assembling an entire puzzle. It all came down to finding the right piece to snap into the right place. With puzzles, the work proves most difficult when all the pieces have the same color. It might take several tries to find the right one, some pieces close but not exact. If one didn't fit right, leaving a gap, it went back to the pile, and the search continued. Like a puzzle, rebuilding the foundation took considerable focus, but it also felt relaxing, almost therapeutic.

"Physical labor stimulates thought," Dan Snow had said.

As the stones moved into place, my mind wandered. The best rocks with the flattest faces went onto the exterior of the foundation. Under a bright sky dotted with occasional patches of clouds, a light breeze blew. The string guided the stones perfectly into position. On the branches of a holly tree, a red cardinal fluttered back and forth watching me. The joints where irregular rocks abutted cast subtle shadows, giving the surface a textured, unrefined character. The bird's high-pitched call broke the silence.

The stonework, now complete, needed sealing to close any gaps that might admit cold air. The cellar still contained some leftover lime putty from the bathroom repair. I mixed a batch of mortar and pointed the foundation just as I had in 86 Main on Nantucket, then filled the trench back in with the earth that I had disgorged from it. Much to Liz's relief, a handful of nails reassigned the deck boards back to their designated slots. In the dim light of dusk, the house sat sturdily atop its revitalized pedestal.

The cardinal had flown away, leaving me, a solitary stoneworker, to contemplate my work in silence. The same feeling of accomplishment at building the rock wall that dammed up the brook as a kid swept over me now. What I had done would last a long time, I told myself.

Six months to go to restore the rest of the house. With spring came a sense of renewal. The days grew longer, and the sun lifted the melancholy that had stagnated in the doldrums of winter. At night, the temperature in the drafty old house hit the ideal level for falling into a deep sleep, leaving me feeling more rested each morning. The land woke, too. Grass greened, and trees budded color into the drab landscape. Many of the wild animals on the property—birds, rabbits, a plump groundhog—were emerging, but the biting flies and mosquitos happily still lay dormant. The house, which I had cursed on more than one occasion during colder months, was winning me over again.

But warm southern air colliding with cold northern air brought violent storms. One pleasant March day, I was sitting by an open window, reading, when in just minutes, black clouds obscured the sun. The room went dark, blotting out the words on the page. A freezing breeze blew through the screen, sending a chill down my spine. Gusts of wind rattled the windows. The intensity of the storm increased. From another room came a faint but troubling sound.

Tap, tap—tap, tap, tap.

VI.

The Window
Wizard

The history of architecture is the history
of the struggle for light.

—*Le Corbusier*

OVER TIME, A SUBURB ROSE AROUND THE Loring property, but pine and spruce trees always kept the house secluded. Their needled bows formed a natural wall. The houses on either side lay a good distance away. Across the street lived our closest neighbor, a seventy-year-old retiree named Art, who had owned a landscaping company. When Lydia Hale no longer could manage routine maintenance around the house, he helped her by fixing creaky doors, hauling heavy garbage bags, and ploughing the driveway after snowstorms. He continued that last tradition after Liz and I moved in. We got to know him and regularly traded favors.

Art was traveling to Florida and asked if we could keep an eye on his house, storing any delivered packages away from inclement weather. We happily agreed, eager to repay him for digging us out the prior winter. Several days later, a large box appeared on his doorstep, and as instructed, I crossed the road to retrieve it. As I walked back down Art's driveway, a new, arresting perspective of the Loring House came into view.

Set squarely across from each other, the large chimneys ascended from each end of the main roof. The second story's five windows appeared in an even row, the center one slimmer than the two windows on either side of it. The sloping lines of the pediment above the front door aligned with each corner of the rectangular elevation facing south, and the windows on each side of that hung in perfect symmetry with those above them. Everything balanced.

In *The Old Way of Seeing*, architectural theorist Jonathan Hale notes that Old World builders obsessed over the geometry in their designs not just for cathedrals and government buildings but also for simple houses. Patterns dictated the placement of doors, windows, stairs, columns, and any other element that might improve aesthetics. You can see these patterns, Hale advises, by tracing straight lines—regulating lines, he calls them—to connect key points of a structure, including corners and the midpoints or edges of door and window frames. The eye relates any element along those lines to the whole in the same way that painters use composition to draw attention to certain features in their work. Hale observes that much modern residential housing often ignores these principles once universally accepted. "When the old way of seeing was displaced, a hollowness came into architecture," he wrote.

A mathematical system based on the Golden Ratio, popular among architects past and present who value thoughtful

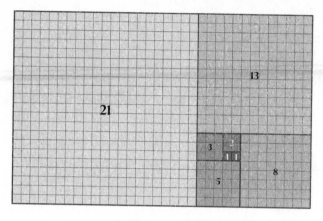

Fibonacci tiling grid

symmetry, holds that shapes with a proportion of 1 to 1.618 look most appealing. If a windowsill runs three feet wide, for example, the Golden Ratio dictates that its height rise to 4.854 feet (3 × 1.618). According to the theory, a window frame with these proportions will please the eye more than a three-by-four or a three-by-five window. The surviving origins of the idea appear in Euclid's *Elements* (circa 300 BCE). Ancient Greek mathematicians studied the ratio, which began as a series of numbers, because it frequently appeared in geometry. Today we call it the Fibonacci sequence. Starting with the number 1 (because 0 didn't exist yet), it consists of a string in which each subsequent number represents the sum of the two numbers preceding it. The first ten numbers of the sequence consist of 1, 1, 2, 3, 5, 8, 13, 21, 34, 55. Understanding how this numerical series became a guiding principle in architecture requires some imagination, however.

When you lay squares with sides equal to the Fibonacci numbers next to one other, they form a distinct pattern. Each larger square combines with all the smaller squares before it to create a repeating rectangle with the Golden Ratio proportion: 1 to 1.618. Followers of the theory spot it everywhere: in the dimensions of a sugar maple, in the spiral of a nautilus shell, in the human body. Architects incorporate it into their designs because recreating these hidden yet familiar natural patterns allows them to project a seemingly divine kind of mathematics and a little bit of ourselves in what they create. The theory crosses a line between science and philosophy, but many architects still swear by the principle. Le Corbusier, a pioneer of modernist architecture, staunchly believed in it. He thought that the universe has a mathematical order, which he described as "rhythms apparent to the eye and clear in their relations with one another. And these rhythms are at the very root of human activities."

Standing in my neighbor's driveway, it was hard to tell whether the Loring House contained Golden Ratio proportions, but its builders clearly had considered balanced geometry when arranging the windows and doors. All of it harmonized. But around the side of the house, which contained the twentieth-century addition, Hale's lament held true. The modern doors and windows had no thoughtful relationship with one another. They looked jumbled. The addition did look less visually appealing than the earlier construction.

AS DARK storm clouds roiled overhead, my attention turned from the book in hand to the ominous *tap, tap, tap* coming from the other room. Wind howled across the pasture, heralding furious rain that blew sideways, hammering the roof. A tree branch scratched at the house as if trying to get inside. The shifting squall jolted it back and forth, its outstretched branches quivering. It looked scared, like it knew what was coming. The real possibility of the tree falling on the house swiftly ushered Liz, Bryson, and me to the ground floor. The power went out, cutting the electricity to the sump pump. The basement slowly filled with water.

Bryson sat on the floor trembling, a worried look in his eye, as I ran my hand over his black fur and told him it was going to be OK. We sat with him, anxious ourselves, and waited for the storm to pass, but it only intensified. In the distance, trees cracked, their gale-severed limbs slamming to the ground. The house's old windows rattled, knocking against their frames. Water streamed down the panes, seeping inside some of them. When the sun set, we lit a candle at the kitchen table and continued our vigil. The faint tapping also continued, followed by a stomach-churning crash that jolted all three of us.

The house had storm windows, but some of them were missing their glass inserts. Others—older than and different from the modern aluminum variety—had wooden frames with two metal eyelets on top that hung from hooks screwed to the house, the storm window fitting over the regular window. An old one had rotted badly, and one of the hooks had separated from the frame. The storm window was dangling from only one hook. The wind battered it against the side of the house, which had caused the alarming sound in the other room. Then a strong gust blew it off completely. Twisting as it fell, a corner caught one of the panes in the regular window, hurling shards of glass across the living room floor.

Rainwater gushed into the house as I raced to find cardboard to duct tape over the hole. After sweeping up the broken glass, I returned to the kitchen and sat crossed legged on the floor with Bryson until the storm finally subsided. The power came back on late that night, and the sump pump gurgled and grumbled to life. The stove clock flashed 12:00, 12:00, 12:00. Liz, Bryson, and I dragged ourselves to bed. Dealing with the window could wait until morning.

Sunrise allowed me to inspect the damage more carefully. Wavy in the old blue-green glass, my reflection stared hazily back from the unbroken panes. Before the storm, the window had nine of them, each pane filled with tiny bubbles, several covered with curves like the grooves of a vinyl picture disc. A decorative pattern adorned the thin, hand-planed strips of wood between each pane, called muntin bars. Some of the duct tape holding the cardboard in place was peeling already.

Made from linseed oil and chalk dust, glazing putty secured the panes to the frame. A putty knife had shaped the material, soft and pliable when fresh, around the outer edge of the glass. Exposed to the air, the putty then hardened in place. But the glazing was deteriorating, and some of the paint covering it had flaked off. A small, off-white piece of putty, hard as porcelain, broke easily from the sash. The entire window needed repairing.

"FEW ELEMENTS of a building contribute more to its architectural character than do the window sash," historian James Garvin posited. With the rise of the Georgian style, the sliding sash first appears in written records from Boston and Philadelphia just after 1700. Before then, window openings had casements. Hinged on the sides, sashes opened outward like cabinet doors. The frame of a sliding sash consists of horizontal rails and vertical stiles. Technology at the time couldn't achieve large, durable sheets of glass, so windowmakers divided frames by adding muntins, which create the distinct grill design still common today. Molded, the inner faces of the muntins evolved over time as architects used them as expressions of style.

Ancient Romans had created molding profiles that the Italian Renaissance resurrected in the 1400s and 1500s. Royal commissions introduced those profiles to England in the first half of the 1600s, and by the 1700s, they had spread to New England with the Georgian style. The standard moldings used in early American architecture had Greek, Latin, or Italian names: *astragal*, *cavetto*, *cyma rectas*, *cyma reversas, ogee, scotia, torus.* The Loring House window sashes mostly used the ovolo profile, a quarter-round separated by a flat band called a fillet.

That winter, Liz and I had joined the board of our local historic society and attended its monthly meetings, which focused on managing three historic properties, upcoming events, and funding for both. Another board member, Pete Baker, owned a small preservation company one town over that, it turned out, mostly restored doors and windows. Eager to make an introduction, I approached him after one of the meetings. He answered a few questions about his company with one-word answers, showing little interest in talking.

"Nice to meet you," he said, abruptly turning away and dashing out the door.

In the days that followed, I emailed him, expressing an interest in working for him. I wanted to learn how to fix an old window, and after months on Nantucket, the prospect of preservation work close to home also appealed to me. "Thanks for the message, but I'm not hiring right now," he replied. "I run a small company and like to keep it that way." His email ended with a peace symbol emoji.

Restoration projects at the house demanded my attention, and the conversation faded from mind. But several weeks later, another email from Baker hit my inbox. One of his employees had left, and he wanted to meet. "No hard feelings if it doesn't work out," he wrote, ending the email with the peace emoji again.

His beat-up black GMC truck pulled into the driveway,

and I gave him a tour of the property, showing some of the repairs that I had done. We discussed his company and the work that he did. That night, another message came. "You know about varnishing old doors the right way? You will soon. Mind-numbing repetitive task of cleaning glass? You will soon." He wanted me to start on Monday.

A short man, Baker had an even tan line above his brow from always wearing a ball cap outside, which divided the luminous white dome of his bald head from the rest of his face. Behind a pair of glasses, his right eye remained fixed, but his left looked slightly off in the distance. A tucked-in T-shirt covered a small pot belly, and from khaki shorts thin legs descended to indiscernible calves. He grew up on the South Shore of Massachusetts and expressed pride in having ancestry on the *Mayflower*. In the 1800s, his family had owned a lucrative mill that manufactured wooden boxes, but the industry dried up, as industries often do, and heirs squandered the wealth. His father died when he was young, and he had a fraught relationship with his stepfather, who owned a tree-service company.

Adults called Baker an old soul as a child because he preferred their company to that of other kids. His mother collected antiques, bringing him with her to flea markets and antique shows to pick through the heaps and hoards. He attended the University of Virginia to become an architectural conservator. While there, he collected furniture left on the side of the road, refinished it, and sold it for beer money. A passion for restoration evolved into a career fixing historic buildings. He had worked on Boston's Old North Church, Thomas Jefferson's Monticello, and the White House.

His shop lay in Halifax, a short drive from the Loring House. The shingled building sat on a triangular lot around which two roads split. A folding table along one road offered house plants for sale. On it, next to a cash box, a hand-painted sign read: "$5 each. Honor system." A large rusty sawblade hung on an outside wall of the building, and stacks of old windows leaned near the door.

Inside, a large table built from two-by-fours and a run-down table saw huddled in the center of the room, filling most of the space. In a corner, a tattered office chair with fabric cushions and a black plastic base sat before an old wood stove. More stacks of windows leaned in all directions, and miscellaneous tools hung from nails hammered into any available wall space. Unmarked containers held colored liquids. Paint cans, buckets, and bottles plugged with rags littered the countertops. The pine smell of turpentine filled the air, and 1970s soft rock played from a yellow boom box. A large Grateful Dead banner hung overhead.

Baker barely said a word when I arrived early Monday morning. The conversation covered basic instructions. A large window lay stretched on the two-by-four table. One by one, he set a stack of small glass panes in the frame. A narrow groove cut in the muntin bars, known as a glazing rabbet, supported each pane. After laying them out, he shuffled to a counter, rifling underneath it for a moment, and returned with a small white plastic bucket. "Elastic glazing compound," read the label on the side.

"This is glazing putty," he said, removing the lid and scooping a baseball-size handful of the material. He handed me a piece. It smelled like new rubber and had the pliable consistency of bread dough. Bits of it stuck to my hand.

He lifted a pane from the frame and set it aside. Plucking small pieces from the ball of putty, he pressed them into the groove of the frame. He worked his way around the opening, set the pane back in place, and pressed its edges. The glass sank as putty oozed from the sides. "First you bed the glass," he said.

A plastic cup on the table contained small metal triangles. He scooped a handful and sprinkled them on the window. "These are points." With the blunt end of the putty knife, he wedged them into the wood on each side of the rectangle. The sharp points dug in like teeth, their ends protruding slightly. They overlapped the glass like tabs on the back of a picture frame. If the putty crumbled away, the points acted as a second line of defense to keep the glass in place.

Plucking more putty from the ball, he pressed it around the edge of the pane, atop the glass. Thumbprints covered the trail of lumpy glazing. With the putty knife at an angle— one end along the muntin bar, the other along the glass—he pushed down, pulling the tool in a straight line toward himself. The metal edge sliced cleanly through the soft material, perfectly beveling the edge. He worked the knife around the entire frame, put a finishing touch on each corner, and looked up. "That's how you glaze a window," he said. "Pretty simple."

It looked easy enough.

From one of the piles against the wall, I took a frame and set it up on the other end of the table along with a stack of panes. I scooped my own ball of putty. The tacky material quickly wadded among my fingers. Trying to pick it off with my other hand only made the situation worse. Putty now covered both my hands. Using the edge of the table, I tried to scrape it off, but, as with a snowball, the mass grew larger, collecting dust and bits of wood shavings. Assuming that a larger ball would gather what was adhering to my hands, I scooped more putty from the bucket. It stuck even more. It looked like I was wearing mittens. Embarrassed, I excused myself from the table to wipe off the mess with a rag.

I was going to need a lot of practice.

The morning progressed with quiet, diligent work. An occasional cough or clatter of windows interrupted the music playing softly in the background, but otherwise the mood remained solemn. In the afternoon, however, the atmosphere changed. Baker came alive, as if a fog had lifted. He regaled me with stories from his past: his experience on a swim team as a kid; his time at Worcester Academy, an all-boys boarding school; dealing with troublesome clients.

In all his tales, he liked to talk about the series of strange coincidences that had occurred over his lifetime. Once, a feeling of foreboding came over him, and later that day he learned that someone he knew had died. He stumbled across a photo of a college friend, no contact between them for years, and the old friend called the next day. At one point, he needed more glass for a restoration project, and someone anonymously dropped a stack of salvaged windows on his doorstep. He took these as signs from the universe, feeling that they represented more than just coincidence and feeling as if, by tuning in to them, he could wield some kind of magical power.

By late afternoon, my glazing skills had improved, still slow but at least proficient. A birdcall clock sounded the hour with the chirpy song of a house wren, which meant four o'clock.

"Time to get out of here," Baker said.

"What are you doing with the rest of your day?" I asked, putting down the putty knife and wiping more putty from my hands.

"I'm going to the beach," he replied.

Baker belonged to the Eel River Beach Club. Every day, he swapped his work boots for a pair of leather Birkenstock sandals and drove his old truck to the waterfront. In his paint-covered T-shirt—garbage bag in one hand, a cranberry vodka in an opaque cup in the other—he walked the shore, collecting seaweed to fertilize his garden, looking less like a successful business owner and more like a vagrant. On one occasion, a woman on her way to the beach saw him and went back to lock her car, he had told me, sounding offended.

Over the next few months, each day played out the

same. Mornings passed in silence while we glazed windows, cleaned glass, and painted frames. Stories filled the afternoons. As I refined my putty-shaping abilities, my thoughts strayed from Baker's narratives, which had started to repeat themselves. How was I going to accomplish my own window restoration project?

I needed glass.

SANDWICH, the oldest town on Cape Cod—the large, curved Massachusetts peninsula renowned for its beautiful beaches, picturesque lighthouses, and little shacks selling fried seafood—once served as a glassmaking hub in New England. The Sandwich Glass Museum, thirty miles southeast of the Loring House, has a studio that still makes glass the old-fashioned way. Curious about its history and wondering whether they made reproduction panes, Liz and I went to see it.

As we drove, towering eastern white pines yielded to stout, shrubby pitch pines. Sometimes called scrub pines, they looked like they had come from a Dr. Seuss book, and they grow particularly well in the cape's sandy, windswept soil. Just across an iron bridge traversing Cape Cod Canal— dug at the start of the 1900s for ships to avoid the dangerous shoals of Nantucket on the original sea route between Boston and New York—stood the museum. From the brick building's wood-shingled roof protruded a large smokestack. A few cars had parked sparsely in the lot.

Inside, everything looked clean, the paint fresh, the carpet spotless. Sitting at the ticket counter, a woman with short, curly, gray hair greeted us and gave us a short history of the museum, explaining that the tours were self-guided. "A glass-blowing demonstration will begin at the top of the hour," she said, handing us each a pamphlet. Just past her, an exhibit leading through a narrow corridor itemized the three materials needed to make glass: silica, potash, and lead. A sample of each material appeared on the red wall along with a description.

Silica—also called quartz, a translucent stone that makes up roughly 90 percent of all rocks on the planet—occurs commonly in New England. On Cape Cod, fragments of it have eroded into small pebbles, forming the sand on the scenic beaches. But early glass producers struggled to reach its melting point of 3,078 degrees Fahrenheit with technology available at the time. They discovered, however, that they could reduce the melting point of silica by adding a flux. Potash, refined from wood-fire ashes and readily available, did the job, cutting the melting point almost in half. But manufacturers still had a problem. Glass produced from silica and potash alone cracked easily. Glassmakers experimented and found that adding lead stabilized the finished product.

Even though Sandwich lies on the waters of Cape Cod Bay, the glass manufactured here came from imported sand. Glassmakers literally brought sand to the beach. They did so because local sand contained a high iron content, giving the glass a tan color, which you can see on the beach and in pictures and paintings of the seaside. Manufacturers used a purer silica sand shipped from the brilliant white beaches of New Jersey. For comparison, the museum displays glass-ware made from the two types, one set yellow, the other clear and sparkling, like before-and-after pictures from a tooth-whitening commercial.

As we were studying one of the exhibits, the woman at the counter shouted across the whole museum, *"The glass blowing demonstration will begin in five minutes!"*

We made our way to the center of the building where a row of chairs, separated by a safety rail, faced a large brick stack. A middle-aged man addressed the room. He had a clean-shaven head, spacer earrings, and a long, braided beard. "Today, I'm going to show you some glass making," he said, inserting a blowpipe into the glowing furnace.

Talking as he worked, he gave a brief history of the ancient art form. He pulled the blowpipe from the furnace, an orange gob of molten glass adhering to the end. Setting it on a flat metal table called a marver, he rolled the glass into a cylinder, then held it out as if sounding a trumpet. "I'm going to trap a little of my breath in the glass," he explained. He blew on the end of the blowpipe, and the cylinder slowly inflated, stretching into a sphere with thin, transparent walls. "I have to keep the glass cool, or the bubble will shoot right through the bottom," he added as he rolled it on the marver again.

At a throne-like workbench with two large arm rests, he sat and laid the pipe before him. One hand rolled it, and the other squeezed a set of long metal tongs against the glass, which wiggled and contorted as it spun. He rolled it back and forth over the arm rests, swapping the tongs for a ladle-like wooden tool pulled from a bucket of water. "This is called blocking," he said, cupping the bowl of the block around the twirling ball of glass. "This cools and shapes the glass at the same time."

He returned to the furnace several times to reheat the piece and then, with the grace of a circus performer, transferred the glass from the blowpipe to a punty—another long metal pipe—which allowed him to shape the glass into a small vase. He tapped it free from the punty, setting it on the marver, and the audience applauded.

"Does anyone have any questions?"

My hand shot up. "Do you make reproduction glass for windows?"

In the 1700s, glaziers used a similar process. Once the glassmaker had blown the holloware, any piece of glass with meaningful depth and volume, he spun it into a large flat disk, which created grooves in each pane. Then he cut it into squares to fit the window frame, each pane varying in thickness. Where the glass connected to the metal rod, the disk flared like the foot of a wine glass, leaving a circular protrusion in the center pane, sometimes called bullet or crown glass.

Like the Saugus Iron Works, the Sandwich Glass Museum didn't have the reproduction pieces that I needed, and no one in the museum knew where to find reproduction window glass for sale. Making it myself crossed my mind, but the only window I'd made to that point offered little practical experience for the job.

Our childhood hikes to The Rock continued into the winter season. Through the snow, knee high in places, we trudged slowly into the forest. Pine boughs drooped under the fresh white blanket. Flakes drifted down and slipped inside the collar of my coat. My boots crunched crusty surface ice into soft snow beneath like a spoon breaking through crème brûlée. The occasional animal track dotted our path before bounding into the thicket.

We stopped at the stream where we had built the rock dam the prior summer, and this time we decided to make a snow structure. We tried cutting snow into blocks and stacking them—to mixed results. Most of the blocks crumbled as we moved them, so we packed the snow instead, sculpting and sloping the walls until the sides connected to form a roof. The dome-shaped structure had a small circular opening, like an asymmetrical igloo. Inside, it seemed more like a cave. Only one person could fit at a time, and it felt claustrophobic. Also, something was missing. The snow cave needed a window.

Along the banks of the stream, a layer of smooth ice had crystalized. We broke off a large sheet, cut a hole in the side of the snow cave, and set the ice window in place. From the inside, the translucent ice revealed tiny air bubbles but blurred everything outside. Light cast a warm glow into the frozen space. The thick walls, creating a barrier from the wind, made me feel secure, protected.

Then the cave collapsed on me. One of the other kids had jumped on it, reducing our efforts to icy rubble, and a snow fight commenced. When we grew tired, we trekked back down the mountain, our footprints the only proof we'd ever been there.

MAKING A window from molten glass represented a much bigger undertaking. Buying the necessary tools, paying an instructor, and renting studio space would cost a lot of money, and time was running out for me to learn a new trade. Buying salvaged glass was another option, but period crown glass was becoming increasingly rare. When updating windows, most homeowners simply throw it away. Asking Pete Baker if he knew where to find any looked like my best option.

"If I have any, it's in the loft," he said.

His shop had a storage space in which he had tucked an assortment of oddities: architectural salvage and various items collected from antique shows over the years. A rickety, handmade ladder flexed unnervingly with each step. In the loft, boxes of old window locks, doorknobs, and hinges collected dust next to a microscope, a pair of leather riding boots, and a machete. In the far corner, in a wooden crate, sat a stack of glass. My thumb flipped through the panes like albums at a record store. Several ancient pieces, tucked under my arm, made the precarious trip back down the ladder. Wrapped between insulation foam and cardboard, the panes also survived the car ride home that afternoon.

The broken window at the Loring House lay sandwiched between the bottom rail of the sash above it and two strips of wood nailed to the side of the frame, called stops. Starting at the top and working with light pressure, my crowbar pried off the stops, the wood bending as the nails emerged. The window slid right out.

Still stuck in the glazing, jagged pieces of glass poked in all directions. Pinching a shard and jiggling released it, like pulling a loose tooth. Most of the glazing came off easily, but in a few spots, it stuck firmly to the wood. Twisting the blade of my utility knife between the putty and frame didn't budge it, forcing me to change tactics. A heat gun blasted hot air on it until the putty melted to the consistency of chewing gum, allowing me to scrape out the rest of the bedding.

On the frame, I set a piece of salvaged glass, larger than the original, and marked the edges. With a ruler as a guide, the small wheel of a pen-shaped glass cutter scored its mark. Hung over the edge of the table, the glass snapped easily in two. A spot check confirmed that it fit in the frame before I lined the thin shelf in the muntin bar with putty. Light pressure around the edges of the fragile concave shape bedded it successfully. I set the points and glazed the outside. The putty knife cut a crisp, smooth line, and the mitered corners, beveled sharp, framed the glass with perfect symmetry.

Traditional finishes used linseed-based oil paint, which I sourced online. The white paint, runnier than its contemporary siblings, needed vigorous stirring to prevent the pigment from settling to the bottom. Dredged up with a wooden stick, the color swirled as it mixed with the dark oil, like heavy cream pouring into coffee. Dabbing just enough to cover the tips of the bristles, a fine-tipped brush applied the opaque liquid in one long, continuous stroke. The paint glided and balanced atop the glazing like a pin stripe.

"You just want to kiss the glass," Baker liked to say.

Rotating the frame allowed me to coat each edge with the same steady movements. I stood back, admiring my work as if I had painted a masterpiece instead of an old window. The sash fit back in place, and new nails resecured the stops. Opening and closing the window a few times confirmed that it worked.

Restoring a window the old-fashioned way seemed like a lot of trouble. The glazing putty didn't last anywhere near as long as many adhesives on the market today. Exposure to the elements made it brittle and susceptible to decay. Over time, it crumbled back to dust. Why did anyone still use it? The practical logic of abandoning window maintenance and replacing drafty wooden sashes with double-paned glass and vinyl made good sense.

But over time, the method revealed an advantage initially obscure. In the material's weakness lay a secret strength. It's easy to remove traditional glazing. Panes can come out with little effort, without breaking. They can be reglazed, and the frame can be repainted. With proper maintenance, an old window can last for *centuries*.

My reflection stared back from the panes of glass as I

reflected on the material's impact on civilization. The invention of glass led to advances in mirror technology, which in turn changed our relationship with ourselves. From the occasional reflection in still water or highly polished, expensive metals, the ability to see ourselves shifted, reshaping our sense of identity, creating, enforcing, or challenging the mental picture of who we are—good or bad. Checking one's or clothing before an important meeting helps when presentation and first impressions matter, but the self-obsession that defines our age can damage our relationships with others. Seeing myself in the window had an impact, too. In a way, I had become part of the house, our identities merging.

With the window restored to its former glory, I returned to the endless parade of small, cosmetic repairs that the house needed, with three months to go until Thanksgiving. For several weeks, everything was quiet—perhaps too quiet. The temperature climbed, and we kept the windows open at night. Warm breezes filled the house with the sweet smells of budding flowers.

But late one evening, another storm interrupted our tranquil life on the farm. As I slept, unconscious to the world, the wind began to whip outside. The windows rattled, but not loud enough to wake me. Then a strong gust shook the house, and something made a terrible sound in the yard. Both Liz and I shot bolt upright in bed, but for a moment it seemed as if it could have happened in a dream.

"Did you hear that?" I asked.

Liz nodded. "You'd better go downstairs."

*Restoring a window the old-fashioned way
seemed like a lot of trouble, but the method
revealed an advantage initially hidden.*

VII.

Brick by Brick

As ye of clay were cast by kind,
So shall ye waste to dust.

—Thomas Vaux

A FEW MILES FROM THE LORING PROPERTY stood another eighteenth-century house, similar in almost every way to my old Colonial, except that it had been slated for demolition. That town's historic commission had put a one-year moratorium on razing the building, but the organization had no other authority to halt its destruction. To placate preservation advocates, the owners put up a fatuous sign in the front yard. "Free House," it read, with a phone number underneath. But with the high costs of moving and then restoring the house—which I intimately understood—they had no takers.

My daily runs took me past the doomed house, my curiosity growing despondent as the imposing structure came down, starting with the chimney. One by one, the disassembled bricks created a heap in the yard. When a large excavator appeared in the driveway, I called the number on the

"Free House" sign and asked whether they would let me salvage any material. Most homeowners don't want the liability of someone wandering a demolition site, but they saw an opportunity to appease the historic commission by telling them that some of the historic building material had found a good home.

On a Saturday afternoon, Pete Baker lent me his dented white van. Filled with a small box of tools, it carried me to the ill-fated house so I could pick at the building's carcass. The place looked like a squatters' residence. Furniture, clothing, and knickknacks lay strewn all over the floors. Rain had permeated the interior, so black mold was growing on the walls and ceiling. Everything felt damp. After studying the architecture for a moment, I went to work, room by room, removing window sash, prying off hardware, gutting whatever made sense. The original wooden bake oven door lay buried in a pile of children's toys until I rescued it. When I had gathered everything salvageable from inside, I drove the van up to the brick pile, picking through the sooty rubble for whole blocks. They stacked in neat rows in the van until the rear suspension sagged. I drove them home, stashing them for safekeeping in the barn.

Over the next several weeks, new construction began on the lot. For a time, two buildings coexisted uneasily, one growing larger each day, while the other withered away. The old house stood solemn, resigned that its time was ending. A new kind of building was replacing it, the technology and materials centuries different from those that had fashioned it. The old house needed a lot of work, but the bones of the place—foundation, frame, roof—all remained in good condition. The owners didn't want to restore it. Then, one day, it was gone.

AWAKENED BY the loud sound in the dark, Liz and I listened intently for another moment, hearing only gusts of wind and window sashes knocking occasionally against their frames. "Whatever it was, I'll deal with it tomorrow," I said, lying back down and rolling over.

The next morning, something strange on the grass was gleaming in the sun. With a silvery, polished-metal surface, it looked like a UFO had landed. The house had delivered so many surprises that little green aliens climbing from the object wouldn't have shocked me. Up close, it looked like a cube, bigger than expected, as wide as I was tall. Then it dawned on me.

To keep water from running into the chimney, someone had installed a metal cap to cover the opening. Vented with grates on the sides, the cap allowed smoke to escape, but the vents also admitted the wind. A gust had lifted the cap like a kite taking flight. The masonry screws let go, and it sailed into the night, crash-landing near the road. A few more feet, and it could have hit a passing car.

The chimney looked much smaller from the ground, but its wayward cap conveyed its magnitude. With little time to fix it, the chimney had to remain open for now. It didn't have a cap originally, so what was the worst that could happen?

Several days later, we found out. The sky unleashed heavy summer rain, and water ran into the flue, pooling on the hearth. Rainwater also seeped through the brick, and brown stains appeared on the ceiling above the fireplace. The chimney cap definitely needed fixing.

The pitch of the roof looked steep, probably 45 degrees. On Nantucket, roofers reshingled a similarly pitched roof for three days, floating nimbly and gracefully along the slope, with no harnesses. Surely, I could do the same. If I could get up to the ridge, I could hoist the cap with a rope and just stick it back on.

An aluminum ladder against a gutter brought me up the two stories and onto the roof, which proved even steeper than expected. I planted myself and leaned forward, taking a few careful steps. My foot shot back as if someone had yanked a rug from under me. Lurching forward, my hands grasped at air as I frantically tried to regain my balance. As I slid backward, bits of sand on the asphalt shingles scraped under my feet. Only the ladder stood between me and the deck some twenty-five feet below. My heart raced as I clung to the ladder rungs, regaining my composure.

OK, new plan.

Borrowing a technique from Michael Burrey, I ordered scaffolding that included a level platform for chimney work on a sloped roof. The body of the frame, made of metal pipes painted blue, used my deck as a base. Planks of wood served as walk boards. A ridge ladder, which lies flat on a roof with a hook on the end so it hangs over the top, helped me assemble the platform, a challenge due to its weight and my fear of tumbling off the roof. When all of it came together, the giant tower of framework loomed next to the house. But lifting the cap still required more hands, so again I put the word out that I needed help and again Aaron Troyansky came though.

He and I hoisted the cap onto the first set of boards, laid across the piping, then leap-frogged it to the next. One of us pushed the silver cube from below, the shiny metal glinting like tinsel, while the other pulled from above. When it reached the eve, we fastened a rope to the cap, careful to keep the braided line away from the cap's knife-sharp edges, and ascended the ridge ladder to the platform around the chimney. At the top, a light breeze cooled the sweat on my forehead, drawing my attention for a moment to the rooftops of the smaller houses in the distance. Looking down, it felt like reaching the summit of Mount Everest.

Painted white, cement plaster covered the large brick stack. Both materials were flaking off in chunks, exposing an earlier render containing tiny horsehair fibers. Sitting, I pressed my back against the chimney. My feet braced against a vertical blue pipe as I pulled the rope. Outstretched, my arms heaved a tug of war with the cap, which inched toward me.

Troyansky, standing on the ridge ladder, followed from behind. When the cap reached the top, we lifted it onto the ledge of brick, then secured it with masonry screws drilled

The chimney cap dreamed of flight
but never made it far.

into the mortar. The threads of the first several screws bored successfully into the soft lime, but as we made our way around each side, they sank and spun. The aging mortar couldn't hold them. Searching for solid backing, we tried drilling new holes, but only a handful of the screws fastened firmly.

"We'll have to live with it," I said. "There's no going back now."

The scaffolding came down, and several weeks passed, bringing summer to an end. The cap held. My work on the long list of repairs inside the house continued. Then yet another storm hit, this time when I was awake. Another strong gust shook the house. Once again, metal clanged a terrible but now familiar sound in the yard. For the chimney cap to stick, the top courses of brick needed rebuilding.

Instinct told me to do the work myself, to jump in head-first and figure it out, as I'd been doing for more than a year. Repairing brick seemed simple enough, and Nantucket had taught me the basics of bricklaying. Surely, I could figure out the rest. But restoring other parts of the house had tamed my overconfidence. A small project on a 300-year-old house could become a big one quickly. This fix called for a professional mason.

Asking around for traditional masons turned up Mike Irons, who agreed to drive down from Maine, where he lived. Middle-aged, he looked like a marathon runner, no trace of body fat, a weathered tan from years in the sun. He wore a T-shirt and an old pair of shorts ripped at the knee, the tattered ring of fabric flapping as he walked. He didn't say much at first, but a quiet intensity burned under the surface. His friends called him Iron Mike.

His father had worked as a mason, and Iron Mike's own career began at age seven, cleaning bricks for a penny a piece. Quickly learning how to use the tools, he worked hard, but no matter how good his work, his father never seemed to approve. "Good bricks," his father said, attributing excellence to the material but not to his son's efforts. Over the years, a feeling of inadequacy built, which unsettled the young man. He internalized his frustrations, bottling them as motivation to work harder. He had something to prove, but the pressure he put on himself and those around him manifested in unhealthy ways. "I was difficult to work with," he said. "I could be a tyrant."

Irons dreamed about leaving it all behind. For a time, he put masonry on hold to earn his master's degree in marine biology. "School came easy to me," he said. After graduating, he packed his car to drive across the country for a new life in California. But his car broke down halfway. As he waited in a dingey mechanic shop in Middle America, he weighed whether to keep going or turn back. "It was a crossroads," he said, "and right then I had a moment of clarity."

Turning around, Irons went back to work with his father. Being a mason, he believed, lay in his blood. For several years, he worked at the family business, but what to do next always hovered in the back of his mind. Eventually he went out on his own. "There's complete freedom to the work I do," he said. "Not a lot of people want to do this anymore, and good masons are hard to find, so people are happy when I show up. You get respect. It makes you feel like you're needed."

From his truck bed, pieces of scaffolding jutted at all angles. Irons wasted no time unloading and setting up, which took him a fraction of the time that it had taken me. He moved across the steep roof, walking the ridge like a cat navigating a fence rail. Chipping away old mortar, he methodically deconstructed the damaged courses. The clatter reverberated through the house below as he stacked bricks in neat rows on the wooden planks. On occasion, wandering into the yard, I looked up to view his progress. My hand blocked the glaring sunlight as his silhouette shuttled back and forth behind the chimney stack.

Guilt overcame me in the kitchen. From the outset, I wanted to restore the house myself, to channel the self-reliant spirit of Richard Macy. Now a stranger was doing the work while I just watched. I didn't like giving up control. The repairs felt like my responsibility. This feeling of unease kept nagging at me, calling me to make my way up the ladder and see if he needed any assistance.

"How's everything going?" I asked after reaching the top.

A long, uncomfortable silence followed. Stone-faced, Irons stared at the bricks. "Fine," he said after a minute. It felt like he didn't need my help, but instead of leaving I pulled myself up farther, poking around the scaffolding. Focused on his work, Irons continued the silent treatment.

He had removed entire sections of brick, and the remaining courses looked like rubble, as if a missile had hit the house.

"Do you need anything?" I asked.

"I'm all set," he replied, tapping a brick with a hammer.

"Well," I paused, feeling a little embarrassed, "I'll get out of your hair."

Irons worked into the evening. When darkness fell, he left everything on the roof and drove home.

"I'm going to need to replace some of the old bricks that have gotten too soft," he said the next morning. "I brought some with me, but I might need more. Do you have any lying around here?"

He followed me to the barn, where the salvaged stack from the demolished house lay waiting for exactly this opportunity. Together, we rummaged, setting good bricks aside. Sensing my eagerness to participate, he suggested that I carry some of them to the rooftop. Then, to my surprise, he opened up. He explained what he was doing and why and gave instructions as I tagged along behind him, up and down the ladder. By the end of the day, I'd become a regular mason's assistant.

MAKING BRICKS begins with clay. Clay comes from stone. When exposed to wind and water or to organic acids from decaying vegetation, stone breaks into tiny particles. When flooded with water, two of those particles, aluminum and silica, bond together. Water also acts as a lubricant, allowing the particles to slide, giving clay its plasticity. Residual clay remains where the original rock lay, while volcanic ash, rain, or wind carries sedimentary clay away, depositing it in places inundated with still water.

But clay alone is insufficient. Stiff and unworkable, clay taken directly from the ground needs tempering in order to hold a good shape. When the Loring House went up, workers dug clay by hand in the fall, setting it out to freeze and thaw with the changing seasons. The piles dried into a crusty, solid mass. To make it pliable again, clay makers spread it on the ground, soaked the material with water, and layered it with sand. Paraded back and forth through the muck, cattle kneaded the silt, their caked hooves treading the material into a paste.

To make bricks, workers first coated rectangular molds with water or sand to prevent the wet clay from sticking, like greasing a loaf pan. Each method imparts a subtly different finish. A water-struck coating produced smooth brick, and a sand-struck coat resulted in coarse brick. The molds sometimes trapped small pebbles or air bubbles against the clay, which left bumps and hollows in the final product, giving each block its own identity. Brickmakers clawed gritty handfuls of the moist earth and hurled them into the rectangular forms. The impact splattered, reddish-brown, everywhere. A straightedge set at one end of a packed mold swept the excess forward the same way that a bartender skims foam from an overpoured glass of beer.

The molded clay, called green brick, airdried before

being fired. Brickmakers stacked green bricks by hand in a scove kiln, a large rectangular structure with corbeled brick arches running through its base, like ancient stone bridges. Brickmasters scoved, or covered, the outer face of the kiln with hardened bricks, layering those with clay to trap heat but leaving openings at the top for hot gases to escape. Beneath the arches, gentle wood fires burned off moisture inside the bricks before brickmasters carefully increased the fires' intensity. If heated too quickly, the water turned to steam, creating a pressure cooker, and the bricks exploded.

Depending on the type of wood, its dryness, and wind drafts, temperatures in the kiln varied from 1,500 to 2,000 degrees Fahrenheit, which affected each brick differently. To control the drafts, skilled brickmakers, relying on judgment and experience, made openings in the kiln's clay face or closed them. But even master brickmakers could control the heat only so well with such crude technology. Bricks closest to the fire blackened, twisting and fusing like metal in a car wreck. Undercooked bricks, called "salmon" bricks for their pink color, crumbled easily. All bricks shrank differently even when dropped from the same mold. After firing, the kiln cooled for several days, and workers dismantled the entire pile by hand. They sorted the bricks by quality, sending them into the world to make foundations and fireplaces, walls and walkways, each with a clear purpose. I had tried wood firing clay once—unsuccessfully.

A hard, late-summer rain in the Vermont of my childhood

had soaked the forest the night before. Beneath the trees, mist still hung in the air. Heavy droplets matted ferns and wildflowers, bowing them to the ground. The trail had turned to mud. Every step that my friends and I took created squelching suction, our boots sloshing and slurping an earthy chorus. Worms wriggled in the saturated soil, rising for air like whales emerging from the sea.

At the stream where we swam, the current had pressed clusters of branches against the rock dam we had made. After the storm, the water had receded from its apex, stranding piles of leaves on the banks, several feet from the stream's edge. Between the leaves and the stream gleamed a smooth layer of satin-sheened sediment, which moss and loam had hidden before the storm. Ochre brown and silky-looking, it smelled faintly of bitter baking chocolate. The gelatinous substance felt cold in my hands. A thin layer of it stuck to my palms, drying quickly and crumbling into dust.

Pinched between fingers and thumbs, the clay rolled easily into a ball, then a shallow bowl. Pocky with fingerprints, the primitive form held its shape. Satisfied with the piece, I set it on a nearby rock, and we continued up the mountain. When we returned, the bowl had hardened, its color a few shades lighter, its surface chalky. We built a small fire, set the crude attempt at pottery in the embers, and waited, ambling by the stream until bored. A stick fished the bowl from the firepit for closer examination. To test its strength, my hands pressed on its sides and applied pressure. It came apart easily, like breaking bread, collapsing into tiny pieces.

I tossed them in the stream, creating and destroying with no discernible purpose, living only in the moment.

As I carried bricks to the roof of the Loring House, Irons lugged two white buckets, one in each hand. Grimacing with each step, he balanced carefully on the ladder as the buckets pulled at his shoulders. At the top, he dropped them on the platform, the plastic landing with a *whomp* as the boards bowed under the new weight. One bucket contained mortar, which he quickly troweled out. The thin metal tool scuffed the hard ledge, slathering the material onto the open section of chimney. The other bucket contained water. He submerged the bricks in it for a moment, setting them aside to dry a little before laying them in a row atop the soft mortar bed.

The new courses took shape, climbing higher. Irons periodically checked them with a level, adjusting the mortar's thickness. With the stack rebuilt, he lined the top of the flue with lime, at times burying his entire head and torso in the hole, smearing the walls inside with a thick coat. The scraping sound of each pass—*scheeet, scheeet*—reverberated upward. He emerged, which enabled me to peer into the chasm. Illuminated by sunlight in the house, only the hearth of the fireplace on the first floor was visible, like headlights down a long, dark tunnel.

Taking Irons's recommendation, we decided to replace the old square cap with low-lying dampers, less likely to catch the wind. They sat atop the chimney, connected to a long metal cord running down to each fireplace in the house. A spring held the tension, which allowed us to open and close the dampers from each hearth. Irons worked on the roof as I went from room to room, poking my head under each fireplace to receive each cord and pull chain. By the afternoon, black soot covered my face. On the last of the seven fireplaces, a long, thin fracture in the vertical courses of brick on one side of the firebox caught my eye.

At some point, workers had removed the bake oven to make room for a closet, but doing that created a structural weakness. Without proper support, the massive weight of the two-story chimney had been bearing down on the thin column at the side of the fireplace, and the bricks were cracking. Irons had to start another job and couldn't help for several months. A sense of urgency, along with the chance to be self-reliant again, convinced me to do the work myself.

Still open to guidance, I reached out to Colin from Nantucket, asking for recommendations on how to start. "You have jacks and bricks and lime?" he texted back.

Repairing the damaged bricks first required supporting the weight of the chimney. Colin assured me that jacks under the lintel, the top opening of the firebox, could do that. Once commonly used to lift houses, screw jacks have a conical shape, like a megaphone set narrow end up. A metal screw, its head the size of a soda can, threaded into the top, which had a hole in the center to accommodate a long metal bar, which a fair amount of leverage could turn. A screw jack that had turned up at a flea market now came in handy.

Hearth, jack, wooden block, lintel—then both hands turned the metal bar. Pushed with one arm and pulled with the other, the screw twisted upward, iron creaking as it rose. The wood block pressed against the lintel, bits of floor grit popping and crunching under the pressure. Spinning the bar took more exertion with each turn until it sat tight.

Accessing the bricks meant removing the planks nailed up to form the closet, which stood in the spot that the bake oven once occupied. Inside a two-panel door with a round white doorknob, my flashlight shone over the rows of shelves dividing the stale-smelling space. Atop each shelf sat old pieces of oxidized newspaper. Some of the browned pages dated to the 1930s. Olive-green paint coated the rest of the space, including walls and ceiling. A hairy spider darted among pieces of bark that littered the floor, remnants of firewood we had stored here that winter. As the shelf planks came out, one revealed a small keyhole in its center, evidence of having served as a cupboard or chest in a previous life.

Behind the vertical boards, the brickwork, once the backside of the masonry behind the firebox, looked less refined than the courses around the mantel. From behind each brick, globs of mortar had seeped and hardened long ago, frozen in messy incongruence and then hidden. My hammer and mason's chisel tapped at a thin string of mortar that had entombed one of the bricks. Pieces broke off in chunks, bits of it sprinkling on the ground as the tools worked their way around it. When the brick wiggled, a small flat bar pried at the ends until my fingers could pinch it, working it back and forth. Slowly, it slid out. The same slow and steady process removed the other damaged bricks.

A canvas cloth on the floor gathered all the rebuilding materials: salvaged bricks, bucket of mortar, bucket of water, spray bottle of water, trowel. The porous, fired clay of the old bricks still in place sucked up spray bottle water until it grew damp, the red brick darkening. My time on Nantucket was serving me well. Too dry, and the bricks would draw water from the mortar too quickly, making it crack. Too wet, and soupy mortar would run, staining the bricks with streaks of white.

The trowel sliced into the mortar, lifting and tilting until the gluey material slid onto the first course of brick. Pressed down, the small pile flattened, and mortar oozed from the edges. The trowel dragged across the top of the hard surface, and then one of the salvaged bricks, soaked in the bucket of water, went into place. Pushed down, the brick sank and stuck to the viscous mortar, like my childhood boots in Vermont's summer mud.

A small gap between the end of each abutting brick allowed a space for mortar to adhere to the ends. Another layer of mortar spread atop the new course. After several hours, the damaged section of the fireplace stood restored. The red fired clay, divided by thin lines of white mortar, added color to the room. The staggered courses of brickwork formed an almost mesmerizing pattern.

A beating heart, the fireplace pumped warmth and life through the house. During cold days, fire drew people close, the flicker of glowing flames calling them to gather, as it had for centuries. Here people cooked meals, the heat providing nourishment to sustain them. It gave them light in the dark, serving as a beacon to guide daily work into the night, helping them survive. For me, it had become a respite where I could settle with a drink, a book, or both, my thoughts dancing around my head like the shadows cast across the walls around me. Sitting in front of the fire brought me peace.

THE END of fall brought me back to my first project in the house: removing the last of the brown paneling from the kitchen. A webbing of old electrical wires that fell from the ceiling, ran over the wood, and disappeared behind the wall had deterred me. The paneling over that section remained untouched until now.

With the kitchen circuit safely turned off, the feathered end of my crowbar wedged between the seam of two panels and began to pry. The nails loosened and the laminate popped. Slivers of veneer frayed into a jagged edge. A cloud of dust filled the air, joined by the bready aroma of aged wood. What was I going to find behind it?

Underneath lay a bird's nest of wiring: some of it covered in braided cloth cord, some of it housed in a ribbed metal tube, some of it wrapped in white rubbery casing. All of it tangled and converged inside a small metal box that looked like a serious fire hazard. My brain tried not to imagine the chaos of an electrical fire on Thanksgiving Day. The oldest wire, insulated with cloth, needed to come out immediately.

It ran up the wall, through small hooks, and vanished into ceiling planks laid across large beams running overhead. In the attic, the other end ran to another junction box. The individual strands gathered inside thimble-shaped plastic caps called wire nuts. A new piece of wire—cut from a large coil bought at the hardware store—replaced the old. The new wire consisted of three smaller wires, one white plastic, one black plastic, one exposed copper, all wrapped together. Twisted into place, they matched the colors of other wires in the junction box.

The circuit breaker, a gray panel with two rows of black switches, lay in the cellar. Sprouting from its top, wires fanned out in all directions, detouring around framing like roadway construction, before slipping into the walls. When I hit the switch to turn the kitchen circuit on, it made a popping sound and ricocheted back to the "off" position. Another attempt yielded the same result.

Huh.

Back upstairs, I couldn't figure out what had gone wrong. Black connected to black, white to white, copper to copper. Everything appeared in good order. Back in the cellar again, another attempt at the kitchen circuit yielded the same result yet again. It popped and shot back off. In twenty-four hours, our guests were arriving for Thanksgiving dinner, and the kitchen had no power.

VIII.

Reflection

It is always our own self that we find
at the end of the journey.

—*Ella Maillart*

THOMAS LORING III NEVER HAD TO WORRY
about faulty electrical wires. Half a century after
Loring had his house built, Benjamin Franklin
famously flew a kite with a metal key attached to the string
to prove that lightning represented a natural form of electricity. But the modern-day electrical grid had to wait until
the 1900s to roll out on a large, useful scale.

A buildup of negatively charged particles, called electrons, creates electricity, a form of energy. It can travel from
a power source to a device, such as a kitchen light, in the
way that water travels through pipes. The light draws power
from an electrical conductor, most commonly copper wire.
Excess current returns to the power source through a second wire that completes a circuit or loop, just as unused or
wastewater flows down a drainpipe.

The current in the wire running from the power source
to the light gives off heat, thus the name "hot" wire, so it

needs an insulator wrapped around it to prevent starting a fire and to protect anyone working with it. The insulator for a hot wire is black. Unused electricity travels back to the power source through a "neutral" wire, colored white to distinguish it from the hot wire. The "ground" wire, a safety measure, defends against unstable currents. If an electrical accident occurs, such as a short circuit, the ground wire channels that unstable current away from the system and outside to a copper stake driven into the ground.

Under the glow of a standing lamp powered by an extension cord run from another room, I was fiddling with these wires, testing different combinations, and running to the cellar to check the breaker. But the result kept coming back the same. The switch popped and jolted back off. After 10 p.m., it was too late to call anyone, so I frantically typed a series of desperate searches into my laptop, grasping for the right words to explain my predicament: "old house wiring problems," "circuit breaker tripping," "breaker switch won't turn on." A link to a page with an accompanying video looked promising, a strange phrase catching my eye: *switch loop.*

In a modern electrical system regulated by building codes, a black wire always connects to another black wire, a white wire to white, and ground to ground. This arrangement helps prevent confusion for anyone servicing that system. Standardization improves safety, but from a previous generation, an electrician working in the Loring House had taken some creative liberties. The wiring for the kitchen

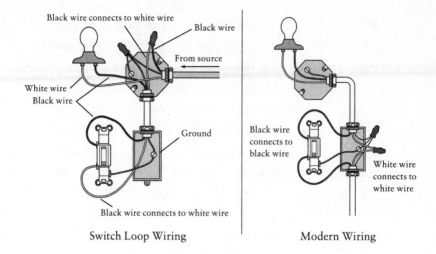

Switch Loop Wiring | Modern Wiring

lights ran overhead in the normal way, but the switch had an unusual variation.

Just like a light, a switch needs hot, neutral, and ground wires. In a modern electrical system, the hot wire runs from the power source, through the switch, to the light. The neutral wire runs from the light through the switch to the power source, which completes the circuit. The Loring House kitchen switch connected only to the hot wire. The black wire twisted onto one end of it, and the white wire from the switch twisted onto the other, a detail that I had overlooked when undoing the wiring. This setup meant that electricity flowed through the switch and to the light, so the white wire was functioning in the same way as the black wire. The switch carried no neutral current. The strange method, called a switch loop, reduces the amount of wire needed to run the circuit. In other words, a cost-saving shortcut.

At first, my brain struggled to wrap itself around the concept, too. The website showed a small diagram of the configuration to explain the idea, but it was making my head hurt. My eyes closed, a photonegative image of the screen pulsing under my eyelids in flashes of white light. Then, from the ether, understanding hit me. All at once, the words on the website made sense. When I had connected the new wire, I matched all the colors, normally the right thing to do. But the website suggested something unorthodox. First, connect the black wire from the switch to the black wire running to the light, then, defying all logic, connect the white wire from the switch to the black wire running to the light.

The logic tracked, but the prospect still made me nervous. As suggested, I changed the wires around and hurried to the basement. Staring at the breaker box, I took a deep breath and hit the switch. It clicked, holding in the "on" position, and a bright light from the kitchen beamed through a crack in one of the floorboards above me. It worked.

THANKSGIVING MORNING arrived with residual triumph from solving the wiring problem. Downstairs, in the dining room, Liz was staring intently at a row of chairs assembled from other rooms in the house. Ignoring my presence, she was counting under her breath, tallying seats to allay a fear that we wouldn't have enough chairs for everybody.

"Can you move the other table into the dining room?" she asked.

As soon as she had spoken the words, car tires crunched over gravel in the driveway. My in-laws, Mark and Dolores, had arrived early to help. Looking like an English gentleman in a tweed hat, knit scarf, and sport coat, Mark shuffled down the walkway. Dolores followed. Her shoulder-length hair bounced with each step, and both hands were clenching tote bags overflowing with foil-covered dishes, extra dinnerware, and napkins.

Liz assigned Mark to help me, so he and I sized up the door frame, which seemed too narrow to admit the table. Looking at it fresh, how had *any* of the furniture made it into the house in the first place? We each took an end and lifted the table, straining under its weight, stumbling forward, trying to keep it from crashing into the walls. As we inched closer, it became clear that the table was too big.

"Let's try flipping it on its side," I said.

We angled it, hooking the legs around the door frame, one pair at a time. It fit—barely. But when we set it down, it rocked back and forth. The table was fine, but the floor underneath was uneven. Some old shingles from the garage, wedged under one of the legs, kept the table from tottering. But when we pushed in the chairs, another issue arose. The dining room floor, built over the cellar, had sagged, creating a huge dip in the center of the room. The chairs on each end of the table sat at a normal height, but those in the middle sank to the floor's lowest point. People in those seats would sit so low that their heads scarcely would poke above the tabletop, like kids at a restaurant without booster seats. We had to improvise. The assortment of chairs had slightly different heights, so we put the ones with the highest seats in the middle and planned to seat the tallest guests in those.

The citrusy smell of the cranberries that Liz was stewing filled the house. The pot lid clattered, jumping as if possessed. Gas flames licked the pot's copper base as steam drifted into the air. The house's old timbers, withered and parched, breathed in the moisture, the wood soaking up the steam.

In the cellar lay some four-by-fours brought from the barn to prop under the floor joists for extra support. Some of the joists had large patches of rot, and the floor might not hold the weight of twenty-seven people. The possibility of it caving conjured images of the *Titanic* sinking, panicked masses in formal wear clambering for their lives among fine food plated on luxurious dinnerware, all of it swallowed into the depths.

With the supports in place in the cellar, I did a quick scan for dead mice, not wanting the smell to ruin dinner, grabbed a few bottles of wine, and headed back upstairs. Liz and I hoisted the turkey from a pot of brine made of apple cider vinegar, slender curls of orange peel, rosemary, pepper, and salt. The wings of the dangling bird spread wide as though it were trying to take flight. We set it in a baking pan, slathered its pale skin in butter, and massaged the butter in before putting the bird in the oven.

In the dry fall air, the floorboards had shrunk once again, pushing their nail heads up like calamitous daisies.

My hammer banged as many as I could find back into place. The wood's shrinkage had widened the gaps between the boards, some openings so large that loose change could fall clean through them. Bits of dust and dirt also found their way in, some of it lodged so well that the vacuum couldn't remove it. The short days and the house's small windows meant eating in darkness, so some lamps were moved into the dining room for extra light. All the woodwork dutifully submitted to wiping that removed a film of mildew. The surfaces near the floor over the cellar turned the rag darker and darker with each pass. We scrambled, sweeping and dusting everything we could reach, though the house never felt totally clean. But that was OK. It had character. The house had made living in it difficult, but we were learning to live in harmony with it.

Mark's cousin Arthur, a retired accountant known for his punctuality, arrived next, holding a potted plant. "I didn't want to show up empty handed," he said, bashfully examining his shoes. Offering him a drink, we ushered him to a makeshift bar assembled on a cupboard shelf.

More cars pulled into the driveway, and soon a continuous procession—aunts, uncles, cousins, and friends with families in other states who didn't want to travel—made its way down the handlaid brick path. All of them carried bottles of wine, casserole dishes, and homemade desserts. We greeted everyone at the door, funneling them into the house, taking coats, and offering drinks.

Austen, the chubby, dimple-cheeked, four-year-old son

of one our friends, stopped before coming inside and looked up at me. "Hi, Uncle Lee!" he said. Perpetually sick from colds caught at daycare, he sniveled and wiped his nose as his father warned us not to get too close.

Reserved at first, our guests congregated in small groups in various rooms of the house. Each cluster consisted of people who already knew one another well. But as the drinks flowed, everyone mingled. The conversations grew louder until stories and laughter drowned out the background music humming from a small speaker set on the hutch. While Liz prepared the food, I gave impromptu tours of the house, as I had with Pete Baker, this time pointing out fascinating architectural details rather than the repairs that I had made.

The table settings consisted of a motley mixture of the wedding gift china that had survived Ruthie the cat's late-night romp and plates bought from a nearby store to supplement those that had shattered. Just before the turkey made its grand entrance, everyone huddled in the dining room. Clinking a glass focused their attention. At the head of the table, I pulled a piece of paper from my pocket. The words on it came from *Of Plimoth Plantation*, which contains William Bradford's account of America's first Thanksgiving.

A native Englishman and governor of the Plymouth Colony, Bradford had no direct connection to me. Most of my ancestors had arrived in America long after the Pilgrims. Working-class immigrants from Ireland and Italy, my forebears had struggled to find their way in a new country. But English colonists had built my house, and Bradford paved

the way for their arrival. That arrival had lethal consequences for the Wampanoag people, who called this region
their home. Those consequences, echoing through history,
still resonate today.

The Plymouth colonists had a fraught relationship with
Pokanoket, the nearby village governed by Ousamequin. A
great sachem, or massasoit, he formed an alliance with the
Pilgrims. For a brief period, the two groups set aside their
differences and came together to celebrate an abundant fall
harvest. Like the Tibetan monks in Lincoln, Nebraska,
the two peoples found peace, if only for a short while, by
living in the moment. Centuries later, the Loring House,
a remnant of that time, still stood, so Bradford's words
seemed fitting.

They began now to gather in the small harvest they
had, and to fit up their houses and dwellings against
winter, being all well recovered in health and strength
and had all things in good plenty. For as some were
thus employed in affairs abroad, others were exercised
in fishing, about cod and bass and other fish, of which
they took good store, of which every family had their
portion. All the summer there was no want; and now
began to come in store of fowl, as winter approached,
of which this place did abound when they came first
(but afterward decreased by degrees). And besides
waterfowl there was great store of wild turkeys, of
which they took many, besides venison, etc. Besides,

they had about a peck of meal a week to a person, or now since harvest, Indian corn to that proportion.

The faces of our closest family and friends all smiled back, and a new thought dawned on me: All my work on the Loring property hadn't been about the house at all. It had been about people.

IN THE cold days that followed Thanksgiving, everything in the house fell quiet. Bryson and I went for our walks. The old black Labrador limped along as we made our way to the blue gate. Unlatched, the hinge squeaked as it swung open. We left the pasture behind and entered the woods. I slowed my pace so Bryson could keep up.

Poking through the thinning canopy, rays of sun illuminated our breath, which condensed and evaporated into the forest. Freshly fallen leaves covered the path. Some drifted down and landed before us. To the right, a rustling chipmunk darted across a log and disappeared into a gap in the stone wall. Turning, Bryson made a feeble effort to chase it but gave up quickly, too old to run. He put his nose back to the ground and kept sniffing the trail.

At the clearing, a deep breath of cold air filled my lungs until they burned, releasing into a sigh. Thanksgiving dinner had been a success. For the first time in months, I allowed myself to relax. A deep, gratifying calm came over me, a feeling that I wanted to last forever—but of course wouldn't.

Tomorrow had new challenges in store, and life would give me reasons to feel anxious, frustrated, or angry. Like fixing the old house, my pursuit of happiness never finished.

As we walked, the events of the last eighteen months replayed in my mind. The restoration had reconnected me to my idyllic childhood, to the kid who lived only in the moment, unsaddled with the burdens of responsibility. Exploring the forest, building crude structures from unprocessed materials, using my hands or basic tools, all of it unknowingly had shaped my future life. Vernacular building and its lack of complication demanded every bit of my attention, swept me up, swallowed me, gave me joy. The work created a mindfulness that cleared my thoughts of all distraction.

For more than a year, the world of preservation encircled me. Long days went into saving my old house and carving out a career in the trades, both aims pursuing meaningful purpose. But the driving philosophy of preservation sometimes proved unpopular. Often characterized as anti-development nuisances, people who believe in saving old buildings at any cost sometimes overlook the human component. Historic commissions halt demolition and delay commercial building projects, often working against the local governments and townspeople that they supposedly serve. America continues to face a shortage of affordable housing, and committees spending *days* squabbling over paint colors are missing that point. Some preservation groups, Historic Boston notably among them, have found ways to repurpose old buildings to meet the changing needs of their communities without destroying the structures, but battles to save properties too often spiral into contention. Despite all that, the work still feels noble to me.

The products of American consumerism are becoming more and more disposable. Fast food comes in a host of wrappers immediately thrown away. Groceries brought home manifest plastic bags that go right in the trash. Small items come packaged in oversized boxes disposed with little concern. With no recycling bin in sight, a plastic water bottle here or there goes into the garbage instead. These habits impact housing as well. Finding cheaper and faster ways to build has eclipsed quality. Materials and techniques used in residential housing today have become less durable than in earlier houses. Why fix a window when you can toss it and replace it with a new one? Why repair fusty old plaster when you can tear it out and put in smooth drywall board? Why restore a house when you could knock it down and build new for a similar cost?

Housing itself is becoming disposable. No longer just for bags and bottles, plastics now go into water lines, shower linings, laminate flooring, countertops, siding, windows, and more. With each remodel or demolition, these non-biodegradable materials accumulate in overstuffed landfills that ruin the landscapes I loved as a kid and appreciate even more as an adult. As the population expands, bulldozers frequently knock down old buildings and encroach deeper into the countryside. They bury marshes and wetlands, suffocating them to make room for yet more housing developments, cramming as many houses into those as zoning laws allow. This expansion affects historic buildings and more recent construction equally. Contractors are creating and destroying at an ever-quickening pace, forming an unlikely metaphysical alliance with the sand paintings of Buddhist monks. In wealthy communities, even the rate of basic remodeling has accelerated. On Nantucket, workers told of homeowners remodeling every five years just to keep up with changing tastes.

Preservation makes a difference. Reviving old buildings with limited resources, making them more energy efficient, rediscovering old methods and materials that last, and incorporating those techniques into modern construction could have real impact. In the face of continued population growth, a revival of traditional building has its limitations, true, but old houses still have secrets to teach us. Their longevity stands, proven. If a building lasts for centuries, materials have more time to replenish. But old houses can teach us and future generations only if they survive. They hold the wisdom of forgotten arts, which we might lose to history without examples to study. They connect us to the past, to our past. The stories of people who lived in our houses before us—what they did, good or bad—helped create our cultural heritage.

A handful of simple tools can accomplish true mastery. Working as earlier generations had, unable to rely on electric motors, took more physical labor, which left me exhausted at the end of most days—but the good kind of exhausted that helped me sleep better. Time spent working this way gave me a deeper appreciation for the house. The scallop in an old beam becomes more meaningful when you've cut one yourself. Rusty iron hardware is worth restoring once you've forged it by hand. A rubble foundation can dazzle once you've stacked one, stone by stone. Throwing away old window sashes, tearing out early plaster, demolishing an ancient chimney stack; these acts became unfathomable after discovering what it took to make them.

The "simple" life rarely proves simple, but the stresses of living in the country felt nothing like those from working in an office. Before buying the Loring House, most of my work took place on a computer screen. Working with pre-industrial technology offered a deeper connection, the points of contact more direct, more sensory. At the house, these tactile materials and techniques created the character that made the house a home. They made it the place where the important people in my life could come together to create the memories that became my own story, this story.

The preservationists I encountered, the people who eschew modern building and choose to live in anachronism, had surprised me. My romantic imagination envisioned a singular community working together with a sense of greater purpose, everyone helping one another, motivated only by passion for the work. Most had no interest in money, other than its necessity to bring projects to fruition. That notion stood them apart from so many people in the financial industry. In books and on social media sites, images of traditional builders made it look as though they had found the secret to living the simple life, somehow tapping into a magic that lay beyond reach for everyone else. The quaint workshops, antique tools, and old wood had drawn me into their world.

But my naïve idea of their community proved wrong. The preservationists I met traveled in packs, divided by an almost tribal cliquishness. They had bitter disputes, which ended in animosity and grudges. People working in stressful, hair-pulling situations yelled and screamed on job sites, some of them dissolving into full-on meltdowns. For every quiet, caring Michael Burrey steward of old buildings, the opposite exists: a narcissistic, disgruntled, or arrogant preservationist who cares as much about money or ego as the purpose of the work. In other words, they resembled every other group of people. My mistake was generalizing about in the first place.

Still, some of them kindly took the time to teach me, sharing their ancient skills, ensuring that their art forms survive, and helping my search for self-reliance as a builder. More than just teaching me technical skills, they showed me how to work by balancing planning and intuition, sometimes letting the project guide me. That balance offered a nice middle ground between the kid who lived only in the moment and the adult who planned an entire year in advance.

The house itself had its own way of teaching me. It taught me patience. With unforeseen problems dictating every move, each project forced me to cede control. Less inclined to

Further proof of jobs well done.
Photo by Liz Bailey.

rush into an endeavor with rash overconfidence, I considered my limitations and assessed situations with better judgment. The process had humbled me. Even my physical appearance had changed, my arms a little bigger from all the heavy lifting, my hair longer, a beard reflecting my new identity.

But on a long enough timeline, both the house and I will go, all the work undone. Looking back, the original question remained the same. Why did saving the house matter?

In those eighteen months, it had become a special place for me—private but not isolated, removed but still nestled in the heart of a dense suburb. Introverted, it still craved connection. It looked the same outside as other historic Colonials and new-construction Colonial Revivals nearby, but it looked different inside. Its state of preservation made it unusual, even a bit eccentric among its peers. Its construction had used basic materials—wood, lime, iron, stone, glass, brick—but assembling and transforming them into a house had required knowledge passed down, from person to person, through the ages. On the surface, it looked simple enough, but a rich complexity lay beneath that. Its vernacular style harmonized with nature, as if, over time, the house itself had become an environmentalist. Properly maintained, it could last for centuries. Left alone, the materials would decompose, reverting into the untamed forest that grew here centuries earlier, little left to indicate that it ever had existed at all. In that way, it possessed immense strength and fragility at the same time. In that way, I saw a little of myself in the house.

In the woods, Bryson and I wandered to the small stream at the far end of the property. He noisily gulped some water, then looked at me with a long string of slobber dangling from his mouth. My sleeve wiped his face, and we headed back. Growing tired, he followed me, nosing the leaves at the trail's edge. A gust blew. He lifted his head into the air and sniffed, eyes squinting, silky ears fluttering. The cool breeze felt good on our faces. We reached the blue gate, and the house came into view once more. It was a beautiful place.

Acknowledgments

THANKS TO—

Liz Bailey for listening to me read every chapter aloud and providing crucial notes along the way.

Leslie Meredith for seeing my potential and signing me as a client.

James Jayo for taking the sometimes jumbled sentences that come from my head, smoothing them out, and making them sing.

Countryman Press for pulling it all together: Ann Treistman, Maya Goldfarb, Allison Chi, Jess Murphy, Devon Zahn, and Devorah Backman.

Roy Underhill for writing an excellent foreword.

Ari Kellerman for the amazing photography on short notice.

Dolores Bailey for always being my biggest fan.

John Cotter, Ethan Gilsdorf, Jessica Keener, Katrin Schumann, Deb Sosin, and GrubStreet for your valuable consulting at the start.

Brian Mandel, Brian Pfeiffer, and Mark Bailey for reading early drafts when this project was getting off the ground.

Acknowledgments

Michael Pollan and Nat Philbrick, my literary heroes, for giving your valuable time to help with this project.

Stuart Krichevsky for steering me to *A Place of My Own.*

Kevin O'Connor, Jon Eig, Kevin Molesky, Jeff Rose, Ultraromance, Jack Lepiarz, Rebecca Lineberry, Dennis Moseley-Williams, Joe Steuter, Neil Menard, Larry and Sophie Cripe, Tim Ehrenberg, Olivia Williams, Matt Breen, Ben Eig, Tom Farragher, and Vin Cipolla for your help or guidance in marketing and promotion and for listening when I needed a sounding board.

Steve Halford for being a lifelong mentor and showing me that a visual artist can be a writer.

Rita Richardson for hanging on to a high school creative writing paper and mailing it to me at the right time later in life.

Michael Burrey for bringing me into the world of preservation.

Dennis McNally, Eric Jay Dolin, Stewart Brand, Val Emmich, Andrew McCarthy, Joel Rose, Rebecca Wells, Matt Arkin, Mary Childs, Serena Zabin, and Tom Putnam for your insights on navigating the world of storytelling.

About the Author

Lee McColgan, founder of a preservation contracting company, has worked on Boston's Old North Church, Louisa May Alcott's Orchard House, and other historic buildings. His work has appeared in the pages of *Architectural Digest*, *Boston Globe*, and *Wall Street Journal*, and he has demonstrated traditional woodworking techniques on *Houses with History* on HGTV and Discovery+. He has given presentations to the Plymouth Antiquarian Society, the Massachusetts Department of Conservation and Recreation, the fraternal organization of Freemasons, and other organizations. He sits on the board of the Pembroke Historical Society and belongs to Historic New England and the National Trust for Historic Preservation. He lives with his wife in Pembroke, Massachusetts.

Roy Underhill is the creator and host of *The Woodwright's Shop* on PBS and the former master housewright at Colonial Williamsburg.